User Interface Design

Jenny Le Peuple
Robert Scane

Computing series editor:
Peter Hodson

Crucial

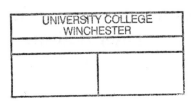
First published in 2003 by Crucial, a division of Learning Matters Ltd.

British Library Cataloguing in Publication Data
A CIP record for this book is available from the British Library.

ISBN 1 903337 19 4

Cover design by Topics – The Creative Partnership
Project management by Deer Park Productions
Text design by Code 5 Design
Typeset by PDQ Typesetting, Newcastle under Lyme
Printed and bound by Bell & Bain Ltd, Glasgow

Learning Matters Ltd
33 Southernhay East
Exeter EX1 1NX
Tel: 01392 215560
Email: info@learningmatters.co.uk
www.learningmatters.co.uk

User Interface Design

Crucial Study Texts for Computing Degree Courses

Titles in the series

To order, please call our order line 0845 230 9000, or email *orders@learningmatters.co.uk*, or visit our website *www.learningmatters.co.uk*

Contents

Introduction
Studying user interface design at degree level

I am always doing what I cannot do yet, in order to learn how to do it.

Attributed to Vincent Van Gogh

This study text is primarily concerned with the study of user interface design and, by implication, HCI (Human Computer Interaction). The aim is to introduce you to the subject area and provide you with further resources so that you can extend your own knowledge by further reading and research. This introduction gives an indication of the range and types of skills that you will need to study the subject area effectively.

The following sections are not intended as a comprehensive guide to 'study skills', there are numerous publications that address these matters in considerable detail and some recommended examples are listed at the end of the introduction. This introduction is based upon experience of the needs of students in this particular subject area and briefly addresses some common concerns.

Resources

Library
Your university library is clearly the best place to find appropriate books and peer-reviewed academic journals. Do not restrict yourself to the sections containing computing, user interface design or HCI material though, because the subject draws from a wide range of other disciplines; Chapter 1, Section 4 gives an indication of these other areas of interest. Make friends with your subject librarian! Contrary to the popular stereotype, librarians do not spend their time stamping books and dusting shelves, nowadays they are **information specialists** and can help you find not only the books, journals and bibliographical indices that you need, but can also direct you to useful websites, show you how to use search engines effectively and find other information resources for you.

Teaching staff
Tutors are not just there to impart 'facts', they will expect you to actively relate to the subject matter. However, your tutors will be only too happy to try to answer any questions you may have and explain areas that you may be having difficulty with. Believe it or not, most lecturers enjoy being asked questions they cannot answer; because this particular subject area is so wide, there is always something new to be thought about by all the participants. One aspect of user interface design that some students have difficulty with is that there is such a diverse spectrum of viewpoints and theory. It is quite possible that individual tutors will favour different points of view and have particular theoretical leanings; eventually you will come to regard this as a healthy state of affairs and not as an indication that 'everyone's telling me something different'. As your skills and knowledge develop, you will be able to hone your critical skills and be able to identify and support your own position on different topics.

Student colleagues
The assessment of your work is likely to be done in absolute, not relative terms; i.e. it is not a competition. It is hoped that all those studying the subject will achieve as much as they

can. To facilitate this, those studying this subject are encouraged to share their knowledge and expertise in relevant areas. If you can help another student of your module to understand an aspect of the subject or to develop a skill in a particular area, please do so. If another student of the module can help you in a similar way, please take that opportunity.

Learning support

It is quite normal to have doubts about your own abilities in terms of the skills that you will need in order to study user interface design effectively. It is a fairly unusual subject area in that you will need to deploy a wide range of expertise. Many of the skills you will have already, or are in the process of developing via other areas that you are studying, but you may conclude that additional help is required, for example with essay writing or whatever. All universities have a department that specialises in delivering additional support to students who feel the need for extra coaching in basic academic skills. There is absolutely no need to feel any sense of embarrassment if you decide to call upon extra tuition to help you succeed, it should be regarded as a positive action. Occasionally, your subject tutors might suggest to you that additional tuition in certain areas might be beneficial, again, you should not misinterpret this advice and regard it as something somehow shameful. Even academics attend workshops and seminars to increase their skills and knowledge! Many universities also have peer support organisations run by and for students.

Internet

The cliché asserting that the internet is a powerful and useful research tool bears repeating here. However, it is all too easy to type a string into a search engine and seize thoughtlessly upon the initial results as being useful to your research. You will certainly be provided with free and fast access to the internet from your university, so you should learn how to make the most effective use of this valuable resource. Your choice of browser is, arguably, not important, but your choice of search engine may be. Most search engines, if you dig deep enough on their sites, explain how they work and this will indicate the type and quality of result you might obtain since they all deploy particular, different techniques; understanding how they work will also indicate the most effective way to construct queries. Whatever search engine you decide to use, or websites you decide to visit directly, you need to make a critical judgment as to the authority and value of the information provided. Some hints:

- when conducting a search, include the terms .ac and/or .edu, this means that the search engine will look for sites in acadmic/educational domains which are more likely to contain dependable information;
- go directly to university websites, most of them have intrinsic search engines that allow you to search within their websites;
- do any of the search results point to professional organisations? Again, these are usually a source of good quality information;
- is there any indication as to when the information was last updated? Neglected websites often (though not always) contain out of date or otherwise dubious information;
- search for the websites of well known authors in the subject area, many of their personal pages contain interesting papers and other useful information and links.

Although reluctant to recommend a particular search engine, at the time of writing (2002) we would highlight Google (*www.google.com*) as being particularly effective since it:

- captures and analyses entire page contents and not just page titles or data in meta tags;
- facilitates a search for particular types of files, e.g. text, images etc.;
- provides a reasonable interpretation of .pdf files into html format;
- provides a language translation facility. Caveat: this can sometimes return some unintentionally hilarious results;
- caches pages so that even if they have been deleted from the host server it is possible to see the original contents;

- is very clear which search results have been 'sponsored' (i.e. the content owners have paid a premium to push themselves up to the top of the search results), these are listed separately over to one side.

Vivisimo (*http://vivisimo.com*) is also worth exploring since it makes a reasonable attempt to categorise the results under different headings.

Yahoo! (*www.yahooo.com*) is useful if you have a reasonably clear idea of what you are looking for and it fits into a hierarchical category, for example computers/internet/games. Incidentally, you might like to look at Chapter 1, Section 3 for an outline of the concept of information architecture.

Note-making

It is strongly recommended that you carry around a notebook (of the paper or computer kind) at all times. You can use this, obviously, for making notes in lectures, tutorials and so on, but also for a variety of other uses, for example to:

- record interesting observations of relevance to user interface design, such as seeing people struggling to use a ticket machine (what particular problems are being experienced?); difficulties you encounter using particular software (how could it be made more usable?) and so on;
- make a note of appropriate sources of information that you find – books, journals, websites etc.;
- make records of meetings, perhaps with team members or others;
- jot down ideas, sketches etc. before you forget them;
- record design decisions (why was it decided to colour this button blue?);
- reflect on your academic work generally.

Tutors often (but not always) provide written notes to supplement lectures, seminars and so on. It is very tempting to imagine that, if you are physically present at a lecture and take away some pre-prepared notes, you have somehow learnt something. Even if notes are provided, you are far more likely to understand and remember information if you actively process what is being said and create your own notes. Everybody has his or her own style of note-making but it is worth experimenting with different approaches. The concept of 'mind maps' devised by Buzan (2000 etc.) is a particular technique that appears to be popular and effective for many students. 'Conventional' note-making generally involves writing text in a linear format, perhaps adding headings to cover various categories of points. There are a number of disadvantages inherent with this technique:

- it takes a relatively long time to write down grammatical sentences complete with verbs, adjectives and so on;
- similarly, it takes a long time to subsequently review these notes, since there is a large volume of text to be cognitively processed;
- take a quick look through previous conventional notes you may have made, the chances are that they are all visually similar, i.e. written in the same colour pen and generally appearing virtually identical, being just pages of writing. This visual similarity makes it quite difficult to distinguish and recall one set of notes from another when you are trying to remember things. It is quite difficult to make connections between different blocks of text to relate ideas.

By contrast, the main characteristics of mind maps are that they:

- contain only key words, not whole sentences (quicker to write and process for recall);
- are non-linear in format;
- are enhanced by the use of colour and pictures (making them easier to recall and to differentiate from notes on another topic);
- make it easier to relate ideas by e.g. drawing in connecting lines, arrows etc.

3

The overall effect is to make the notes highly personalised, since they represent **your** view of a topic. If you are interested in developing the technique of mind maps, it is recommended that you consult one of the many sources on the subject, since only an extremely abbreviated and simplified explanation has been presented here. In the meantime, to give you the general idea, you will see below in Figure 0.1. a preliminary – and incomplete – mind map that was drawn in connection with Chapter 1 of this book (note: it is only reproduced in black and white). When you study Chapter 1 yourself, have a go at producing your own mind map – it will probably look quite different from Figure 0.1 and will therefore have particular significance for **you**. Needless to say, if you find this method of note-making doesn't work for you, then stick to your preferred method or look elsewhere for other inspiration.

Figure 0.1 Author's mind map of Chapter 1

Reading

This may seem obvious, but you will derive more benefit from your research if you try to develop your reading skills. The study of user interface design necessarily involves much reading and research using books, academic journals and other written material. One of the ways to learn how to **write** well is to **read** well and widely. In general, the **more** you read the better, but try to be selective about **what** you read; a steady diet of tabloid newspapers and popular magazines is unlikely to help you increase your vocabulary or learn to recognise and emulate good quality writing. Most Student Union shops sell broadsheet newspapers at reduced prices, and libraries always have an extensive selection of current newspapers and interesting periodicals.

It was mentioned earlier that there exists a wide diversity of viewpoints within the interface design community. Whatever you are reading, try to develop the habit of critical thinking. Cottrell (1999) notes that:

Critical thinking when reading involves the following:

- **identifying** the line of reasoning in the text;
- **critically** evaluating the line of reasoning;
- **questioning** surface appearances and checking for hidden assumptions or agendas;
- **identifying** evidence in the text;
- **evaluating** the evidence according to valid criteria;
- **identifying** the writer's conclusion/s;
- **deciding** whether the evidence presented supports the conclusion/s.

(our emphases)

It can be daunting to be faced with a sizeable choice of journals and books in the library – where to start? Some ideas:

- reading lists and references provided by your tutors;
- a bibliographic index appropriate to your subject area, many of which are available online nowadays (the librarians will help with this);
- references and bibliographies in books and academic papers;
- books and papers written by an author with whom you are already familiar.

Get into the habit of scanning titles, contents pages, abstracts and indices to get an approximate idea of whether the source is going to be useful for your purposes. If the book or paper that you are reading belongs to you, there is nothing wrong with scribbling notes in the margins, highlighting important areas and so on – this will help you with making your own notes.

Some of our students comment that such and such a paper is 'too difficult' or 'I had to read it more than once'. Many papers worth investigating **are** difficult to understand at first read; even seasoned academics have to read things several times to gain a full understanding of the content. It is only with the practice of reading progressively difficult material that illumination occurs.

Writing

General points
As with reading, writing skills develop with regular practice. Get into the habit of writing **something** in your notebook (in your own words) every day, even if it amounts to just a page or so. When it comes to writing up a report or an essay it will then not feel quite so frightening to be faced with a blank sheet of paper or empty word processing document.

Cultivate the practice of writing in an academic style; your tutors will not appreciate assignments expressed in an informal manner and you will probably lose marks for this approach. Do not rely heavily on spell-checkers – for example my word processing software happily accepts 'spool-choker' even though it is a nonsense word. Make use of a good quality thesaurus to extend your vocabulary. Accurate spelling and grammar are **important**; think of them as being a protocol for communication in much the same way that computers need protocols to communicate properly. If your spelling and grammar are up to scratch, you have a much better chance of conveying your ideas precisely; it is not much use having good ideas if you are unable to convey them unambiguously to others.

Your assignments are likely to include essays and reports, both of which require a different approach and format. Before you embark on either, read the instructions carefully and take note of aspects such as word length and content; for example, most report-style assignments will have very specific guidance as to the exact content required such as section names and so on. **Check with your tutor if there is anything that you don't understand**.

In the field of user interface design you will often be called upon to write up a particular activity that you have been engaged in, for example a requirements gathering process or a design exercise. As well as the actual **outcome** of these types of activities, your tutor will want a full account of the actual **processes** involved. For example, in the case of evaluating an interface (see Chapters 6 and 7) you would probably need to provide details of:

- why (aims, objectives …);
- who was involved (the design team, subjects …);
- when (dates, times …);
- where (computer laboratory, subjects' workplace …);
- what techniques (discussion of techniques available, rationale for choice …);
- what materials were used (questionnaires, computers …);
- what was actually done (observed people, interviewed them …);
- raw results (times taken to complete tasks by each subject, completed questionnaires …);
- summary of the results (charts, graphs, tables …);
- your interpretation of the results (what does all the data mean? and why?);
- possibly a reflective critique of how things went (what techniques were useful/not useful, how problems within the team were resolved etc.).

And so on.

By including this type of information, the reader will have a clear picture of **how** and **why** you arrived at a particular conclusion. It will demonstrate your knowledge of particular techniques, your skill at deploying those techniques and your ability to make rational decisions and provide support for those decisions.

Presentation of work

Hopefully you would not dream of handing in assignments handwritten on scruffy bits of paper, complete with crossings-out and other amendments. Undoubtedly this is how your work will start out, and often it is perfectly in order to include, perhaps, a workbook containing background documentation which might include scribbled notes, rough drawings and so on. For submitting finished work though, it is well worth taking the trouble to word-process your assignment, taking care that:

- it is in the correct style (essay, report etc.);
- there is a contents page;
- the formatting is appropriate (consistent and appropriate layout, font style and size etc.);
- there are page numbers;
- there are appropriate sections and sub-sections (if it is a report);
- it is appropriately illustrated if necessary, with charts, diagrams etc. (do, please, avoid using tacky clip art);
- it includes a references section;
- supporting, background information is contained in appropriate appendices;
- the pages won't fall apart (a simple and obvious point perhaps, but you don't want to run the risk of losing bits of your work).

By complying with the above points, your assignments will demonstrate that you are proud of your efforts and the document will look inviting to the assessor.

Using references

An important part of writing in an academic style is the correct use of citations, references and bibliographies; it is **essential** to acknowledge and specify the sources of your information and ideas. Most study skills books explain in some detail how to do this properly, and your university's library and/or website are sure to have plenty of information on this topic. Some definitions:

- A **citation** is where a source is stated in the body of the text e.g. 'Nielsen (1993) further suggests that ...' or '... example from Gerhardt-Powals (1996) uses empirical research ...'.

- Where a citation has been used, there should be a corresponding **reference** in the references section at the end of the text. Using the above as examples, you will find:

  Nielsen, J. (1993). *Usability Engineering*. AP Professional.

  and

  Gerhardt-Powals, J. (1996). Cognitive engineering principles for enhancing human-computer performance. *International Journal of Human-Computer Interaction* 8, (2), 189–211.

  in the references section at the end of this book. One would not expect to find references within a reference section that had no corresponding citation in the text and vice versa; **do not be tempted to append an impressive looking array of references if they are not cited in the text, and do not use citations without a corresponding reference.**

- A **bibliography** is where you can list sources that are not directly cited. A bibliography usually contains references that indicate general background reading that is not specifically cited. In some texts you will find a bibliography, rather than a references section that also includes specific citations.

- **URLs** – using websites for reference is a relatively modern phenomenon, for obvious reasons, and so there is no generally agreed format. You should, however, include as a minimum: the author's name (if known); the date it was published (if known); the title of the web page if it has one, or failing that, a clear identifier as to what it is; the full URL; the date it was last looked at (bearing in mind that some pages change frequently and may contain different information next time they are accessed).

Note the different formats shown above for the journal and the book – again, consult a reputable source for details of how to format different types of references. Check with your tutor whether a bibliography or references section (or both) is required for a particular assignment.

It is good practice to keep the details (author, date, title, publisher etc.) of any interesting sources that you come across together with a brief description of the information they contain. You could keep your references in a card index or perhaps in a computer database.

Avoiding plagiarism

Plagiarism is, to put it bluntly, a form of **cheating**. A more formal definition of the verb **plagiarise**, taken from *The Concise Oxford Dictionary* (1995) is:

'1. take and use (the thoughts, writings, inventions, etc. of another person) as one's own. 2. pass off the thoughts etc. of (another person) as one's own ...'

All academic institutions take plagiarism and cheating of any kind very seriously – Note: tutors are usually expert at detecting plagiarism and cheating and most institutions do not hesitate to impose severe penalties on those found guilty. So, how can you avoid being accused of plagiarism?

- Do not simply cut and paste information from the internet or copy text from paper sources. Everything you write should be in your own words. It is not enough simply to paraphrase text or change a few words; apart from the plagiarism aspect, this approach would demonstrate insufficient processing of the information.
- *Always* acknowledge sources of ideas by using citations and references correctly.
- If you do wish to include a direct quote, make it obvious that it **is** a quote by enclosing it in quotation marks and/or italicising it. Make sure that the source of the quote is clearly stated by way of a citation. Incidentally, an assignment composed almost entirely of direct quotes would not be received at all favourably; your tutors will want to read about **your** ideas, written in your own words.
- Last, but by no means least, **never, ever** feel tempted to copy anything from your fellow students.

Recommended reading

Books

General study skills
Buzan, T. and Buzan, B. (2000). *The Mind Map Book*. BBC Consumer Publishing (Books).
Cottrell, S. (1999). *The Study Skills Handbook*. Macmillan.
Dawson, C. W. (2000). *The Essence of Computing Projects: A Student's Guide*. Prentice Hall.
Race, P. (1999). *How to Get a Good Degree*. Open University Press.

Specific to user interface design
Norman, D. A. (1998a). *The Design of Everyday Things*. MIT Press. (Originally published in 1988 as *The Psychology of Everyday Things*, Basic Books.) A classic publication – recommended reading at the outset to really get you thinking about the subject.

All of the following are cited frequently in the main text, and much of the further reading at the end of the chapters is directed towards these publications.

Dix, A. J., Finlay, J. E., Abowd, G. D. and Beale, R. (1998). *Human Computer Interaction*, 2nd edition. Prentice Hall.
Faulkner, X. (2000). *Usability Engineering*. Macmillan Press Ltd.
Nielsen, J. (1993). *Usability Engineering*. AP Professional.
Newman, W. M. and Lamming, M. G. (1995). *Interactive System Design*. Addison-Wesley.
Preece, J., Rogers, Y., Sharp, H., Benyon, D., Holland, S. and Carey, T. (1994). *Human-Computer Interaction*. Addison-Wesley.
Preece, J., Rogers, Y. and Sharp, H. (2002). *Interaction Design: Beyond Human Computer Interaction*. Wiley.
Shneiderman, B. (1998). *Designing the User Interface*. Addison-Wesley.

Academic journals

This is just a brief selection of the many journals that are appropriate to the study of user interface design:

- *International Journal of Human-Computer Studies*
- *Interacting with Computers*
- *Human-Computer Interaction*
- *Behaviour and Information Technology*
- *Ergonomics*
- *Human Factors*

Websites

There are far too many to list all of them here, but the following are useful places to start and are not likely to 'disappear'.

ACM SIGCHI. *http://www.acm.org/sigchi* The Computer-Human Interaction Special Interest Group of the Association for Computer Machinery.

BCS HCI (The British HCI Group). *http://www.bcs-hci.org.uk* The HCI specialist group of the British Computing Society.

HCI Bibliography. *http://www.hcibib.org* A comprehensive and well-maintained site authored by Gary Perlman who is an information scientist currently conducting research at the OCLC (Online Computer Library Center).

Usability News. *http://www.usabilitynews.com* The 'sister' site to the BCS HCI group.

UK UPA. *http://www.lboro.ac.uk/research/esri/hfdc/ukupa* The UK chapter of the Usability Professionals' Association (see below).

UPA. *http://www.upassoc.org* Usability Professionals' Association.

Note: there are special student rates available to join SIGCHI, BCS HCI and the UPA.

Chapter 1
Background: the nature, importance and scope of usable interfaces

Chapter summary

It is relatively easy to design and build IT systems that work in the sense that they perform all the desired functions without error. But however functional a system is, it is of little value if the intended users are unable to access all this functionality. The user interface is the part of a system that actually enables people to interact with the underlying technology – usability and functionality contribute equally to the overall acceptability of a system. This chapter provides some background to the design of high quality user interfaces; later on in the book you will see **how** to design interfaces that people enjoy using and which enable them to use a system effectively.

Learning outcomes

Outcome 1: Understand what is meant by the term user interface and explain different models.
You will need to demonstrate that you understand what is meant by the term user interface, understand the general concept of models and be able to explain various models of interaction. Question 1 at the end of the chapter tests your understanding of these ideas.

Outcome 2: Explain what is meant by usability, why it is important and where it fits into overall system acceptability.
You need to be able to explain different definitions of usability and why system usability is an important factor in overall system acceptability. Question 2 at the end of the chapter assesses your ability to explain the idea of usability.

Outcome 3: Identify the scope of a user interface design project.
When designing an interface, you should be able to identify and take account of a range of important factors. Question 3 at the end of the chapter gives you an opportunity to think about these factors.

Outcome 4: Demonstrate an awareness of the disciplines that underpin interface design.
You should be aware of the wide range of disciplines that contribute to the study and practice of interface design and be able to explain **how** they contribute. Question 4 at the end of the chapter tests your understanding of this.

How will you be assessed on this?

In order to understand user interface design you will have to have a clear understanding of what a user interface **is** and some knowledge of well-known models of human computer interaction. For practical work, you will need to understand what is meant if you are asked to design the interface to a system. In an examination you may be asked to explain what is meant by 'interaction' or 'interface' and you may be asked to describe or explain different models of human computer interaction. You might be directed to critically evaluate a particular model, or compare and contrast different models. In order to design a usable interface, you will need to have a clear understanding of what usability **is**, be able to recognise poor usability and have an idea of the factors that contribute towards **good** usability. You will need to be able to start identifying specific usability problems that will have to be overcome and start to consider how you might evaluate the success of your design. You may be asked to demonstrate that you understand the importance of usability, both to individual users and in a business environment. You may need to explain why system usability is as important as system functionality. In an examination, you could be asked to discuss various definitions of usability and why usability is important.

As part of the interface design process, you will need to identify and take into account a wide range of factors such as the characteristics of the users or the range of disciplines that contribute to interface design ; you may be asked in an examination to explain and discuss these types of factors.

Section 1

What is a user interface?

In this section we will discuss various definitions of the term user interface, look at two particular models and arrive at an overall understanding of the term.

Imagine that you are sitting down to write a letter to your bank manager (to ask for an increase in your overdraft!). You could either write it out by hand using a pen and paper or, perhaps to make it look professional and to keep a record of the communication, you could word process the document. In either case, your objective is the same – to write a letter; at a higher level, your overall aim, of course, is to secure some additional cash. Whichever method you choose will involve a series of tasks deploying some kind of tools to achieve your objective. In the first case, the tools would be a pen and writing paper, in the latter, a PC (loaded with some word processing software) and a printer. Both sets of tools can be thought of as writing systems. The point here is that you are not using either system just for the sake of it, each is simply a means to an end. It should also be borne in mind that you might use different systems for different purposes; if you were, for example, writing a letter of condolence, you might conclude that a hand-written letter would convey a more personal effect.

CRUCIAL CONCEPT

An **aim** is a high level goal that is achieved by meeting a series of objectives that could involve completing tasks with the various tools that make up a system.

CRUCIAL TIP

Sometimes you will find the term **goal** used interchangeably with **aim** or **objective**.

CRUCIAL TIP

Start thinking about the series of **tasks** that are involved in writing a letter – later on in the book we will be looking at **task analysis**.

Think about what is involved in writing with a pen and paper system. Imagine if the pen was a metre long, 50cm in diameter and was covered in a spiky material. And what if the paper was so absorbent that it immediately sucked all the ink out of the pen? If this were the case, this particular system would clearly be unusable; you would not only be unable to write the letter, but it would also be a most unenjoyable experience. The problem here lies with the user interface – the properties of the pen and paper that allow the user to interact with the underlying technology.

CRUCIAL CONCEPT

A **user interface** is the point of contact that enables an interaction between a human being and a system.

CRUCIAL TIP

An **interface** is not just the point of contact between a human and a **computer** system, even relatively simple artefacts like doors have an interface!

A well designed system, whether it be pen and paper or a word processor, would enable you to write that important letter easily and effectively. Such a system could be said to be usable and so would demonstrate some degree of usability. There are many definitions of the word 'usability' and we will be looking in more detail at the concept later on in Section 2.

CRUCIAL CONCEPT

For now, we will simply describe **usability** as a measure of the quality of a user's experience when interacting with a system.

CRUCIAL TIP

Sometimes the phrase **user friendly** is used to describe a system that has a high degree of usability. Many companies like to advertise their products by claiming that they are user friendly.

It is useful to try to model what is going on inside both computers and humans and the interactions between the two; many such models have been proposed. At this point we should be clear, in the context of this book, about what is meant by 'models' and why they are valuable. You are probably all familiar with the idea of a **physical** model, for example a model boat or an architect's model of a building. Physical models are generally (though not always) a literal and concrete representation of a 'real' object reproduced to a lesser or greater degree of accuracy and detail. What is generally termed a **conceptual** model, on the other hand, is the representation of an **idea** of how something might work in order to try to understand it. The main characteristics of most models are that they:

- are a **representation** of how something might work and help offer **explanations**;
- are generally **incomplete** in that they only include **essential** features;
- can be used for the purposes of **prediction**.

In this book, 'model' will generally refer to conceptual models – the two examples of interaction models outlined in this section (below) will help you understand the term better. In later sections of this book, you will come across other instances of models.

CRUCIAL CONCEPT

A **model** is a representation that attempts to explain the essential features of how something might work. Models are sometimes used to predict the outcome of, for example, making a change to some component of a system.

So, why do humans interact with systems? And how? One technique for exploring these types of complex questions is to build models. One of the best known and most durable models of human computer interaction is that proposed by Donald Norman (1988a) known as the 'execution – evaluation cycle'. In Norman's own words:

To get something done, you have to start with some notion of what is wanted – the goal that is to be achieved. Then, you have to do something to the world, that is, take action to move yourself or manipulate someone or something. Finally, you check to see that your goal was made.

The cycle as modelled is divided into seven stages of action, one phase for goals, three for execution and three for evaluation:

- forming a goal (what is the desired outcome?);
- forming an intention (preparing to act so as to achieve the goal);
- specifying the action (what action/sequence of actions have to be performed);
- executing the action (initiating the actions);
- perceiving the state of the system (observing what has happened);
- interpreting the state of the system (what has **actually** happened);
- evaluating the outcome (is this what was **expected** to happen?).

Although this model appears to be neat and tidy, as Norman points out it is an 'approximate model', the stages are not necessarily discrete, the processes can be started at any stage, people may loop round and round and change their goals (or not even have clear goals to start with). This illustrates what was said earlier about models being a representation of the salient features of something rather than being exactly analogous.

CRUCIAL TIP

Bearing in mind that that both systems and humans are involved in an interaction, what is missing from Norman's model?

CRUCIAL CONCEPT

Norman's **execution-evaluation cycle** is a model of human computer interaction that focuses on the **human** view of the interaction.

Abowd and Beale (1991) later extended Norman's model to incorporate the system view – 'a general interaction framework', this is illustrated below, in Figure 1.1.

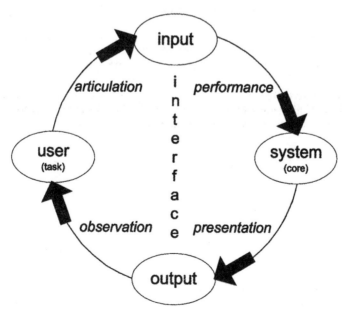

Figure 1.1 General interaction framework, after Abowd and Beale, 1991

In this model, the four main components are the **user**, the **system**, the **input** and the **output**. Together, **input** and **output** form the **interface.** Each of the components has its own 'language'. In this model, there are four steps in an interaction:

- **articulation**: the user initiates the cycle by formulating a task to achieve a goal and articulates this task via the input language;
- **performance:** the input language is translated into the system core language and transmitted to the system, the system responds by transforming itself into a different state;
- **presentation**: the new state of the system is communicated to the user;
- **observation**: the user observes the output and assesses the results in terms of the original goal.

CRUCIAL CONCEPT

Abowd and Beale's **general interaction framework** is a model of human computer interaction that incorporates both the human and system aspects of an interaction via the interface.

CRUCIAL TIP

Models are useful for exploring difficult ideas and they can help to visualise problem areas. Models are not necessarily expressed in a graphical way i.e. in a diagrammatic format.

Quick test

1. Give your own definition of the phrase 'user interface'.

2. Explain what is meant by a 'model'.

3. Outline Norman's execution-evaluation cycle.

Section 2

Usability

In this section we will cover usability in more depth by examining some of its attributes, considering how it might be measured, explaining why usability is important and seeing where usability fits into general system acceptability.

It was mentioned earlier that usability was an important attribute of an IT system, and one particular definition was introduced. In fact there are many definitions of usability, for example:

> The extent to which an end-user is able to carry out required tasks successfully, and without difficulty using the computer application system.
>
> (Ravden and Johnson, 1989)

Or, more specifically,

> Usability: the extent to which a product can be used by specified users to achieve specified goals with effectiveness, efficiency and satisfaction in a specified context of use.
>
> (ISO 9241-11: Guidance on Usability, 1998)

CRUCIAL TIP

ISO stands for the **International Organisation for Standardisation**; we will be covering standards in Chapter 3.

The term 'user friendly', as mentioned earlier, is considered by many to be imprecise and unquantifiable, by contrast the term 'usability' has come to imply that certain qualities of the interface are more specific and measurable. Nielsen (1993) takes the view that usability has multiple components and has identified five key attributes:

- **learnability**: a system should be easy to learn so that users can quickly start to use it;
- **efficiency**: once the user has learned how to use the system, it should support a high level of productivity;
- **memorability**: if a user returns to the system after a period of not using it for a while, it should not be necessary to re-learn how to use it;
- **errors**: the system should be as error free as possible, make it possible to recover from errors and prevent catastrophic errors from occurring;
- **satisfaction**: users should find the system subjectively pleasing to use.

Obviously, the above attributes, which can be thought of as principles, are very high level; they indicate to interface designers what to aim for in a very general way but do not give us much idea about how precisely an interface can be designed so as to be usable – what is needed are more specific guidelines. In his book, Nielsen goes into a great deal of detail about what constitutes usability, how to design to ensure usability and how to evaluate the extent of a system's usability – hence the title: *Usability Engineering* – a clear indication that good usability doesn't just happen by accident! Later on in this book in Chapter 3 we will be discussing usability principles and guidelines, the relationship between them, and why and how interface designers might use them.

CRUCIAL CONCEPT

Usability is a measurable property and comprises many attributes. Interface design/usability experts often have differing ideas about what these attributes are.

The point about thinking about usability in terms of having particular attributes is that that usability can be **measurable**. The interface designer should identify clear usability goals (which can be based on usability principles) early in the design process as part of the requirements gathering stage. When specific and measurable usability goals are established, the system can then be evaluated to establish the extent to which these goals have been met. Evaluation is a **key** process in interface design and will be considered in detail in Chapters 6 and 7.

Establishing usability and other design goals will be covered in Chapter 4, but let us briefly look now at a quick example. Imagine that you are designing a commercial website for a manufacturer that specialises in clothing for older people; the intention is that customers should be able to view a catalogue and order items online. Some typical goals could include:

- the pages load quickly (the designer could aim for a precise time, but of course the speed of web access is subject to all kinds of variables which are outside the control of the designer. But the designer could, for example, aim to make the pages smaller – in terms of file size – than existing ones);
- the text is always visible against the background (this would apply to all websites, naturally, but is particularly important if the target audience comprises older people, who may have less acuity of vision).

You should be able to see from these examples that the website could be evaluated to see whether the usability goals have been met.

CRUCIAL CONCEPTS

Usability goals should be specific and measurable. **Interfaces** can be evaluated in order to determine the extent to which usability and other design goals have been met.

By now, you should be forming an idea as to why usability is an important feature of IT systems. Apart from enabling individuals to use systems effectively and enjoyably, which is an important aim in itself, there are also numerous business benefits to be accrued by organisations from deploying systems that are usable.

Here are some clear and measurable benefits of usable systems:

- efficiency – quicker to use, need less keystrokes etc.;
- effectiveness – work tasks and goals are achieved more successfully;
- productivity – self explanatory I hope;
- safety – it is **essential** for safety critical systems to be usable, for example: aircraft cockpit displays, the controls in a nuclear plant;
- user satisfaction – employees who do not have to wrestle with unusable systems are less likely to become stressed, ineffective or sick.

CRUCIAL TIP

Efficiency generally means that resources such as time and labour are kept to a minimum while carrying out business processes. **Effectiveness** generally means that the processes have the desired overall result.

One of the large UK banks produces much of its business software in-house and has its own, specialist usability services department. The purpose of this department is to ensure that the IT products used both by employees and by customers (for example automatic teller machines) are usable. The usability services department identifies the following, very tangible benefits of engineering usability:

- improved image to users (of the IT department);
- higher quality end product;
- lower costs over lifetime of product;
- lower initial/on-going training costs;
- improved user efficiency/accuracy;
- lower help-desk costs.

CRUCIAL CONCEPT

Usability is important because systems that have a high degree of usability can ensure tangible and measurable business benefits.

Right at the beginning of this chapter it was intimated that usability was part of overall system acceptability. Figure 1.2, below, is adapted from Nielsen (1993) and illustrates very clearly where usability fits into the whole picture. Incidentally, it is another example of a model.

CRUCIAL CONCEPT

Usability is a key component of overall **system acceptability**.

You will see from Figure 1.2 that are many aspects of a system that are important to get right in order for a system to be acceptable to the user. Some of them you are probably already familiar with, for example the idea of the system's utility, i.e. does it perform the functions it is intended to do, and perform them correctly? One way of establishing a system's utility, or functionality, is by subjecting the system to various types of testing such as the 'black box' and 'white box' types of techniques. While it is obviously important that a system functions correctly and accurately, this type of testing is outside the scope of this book – we will be looking instead at how a system's usability can be evaluated.

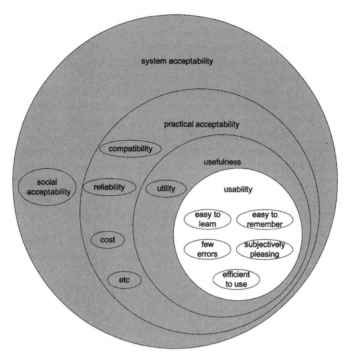

Figure 1.2 Model of the attributes of system acceptability

Quick test

1. Give your own definition of usability.

2. According to Nielsen, what are five key attributes of usability?

3. Why is system usability important to business organisations?

Section 3

The scope of user interfaces

It is easy to think of an interface as simply consisting of what might be included on a screen display – the icons, buttons etc. This section introduces some of the other aspects that need to be considered when designing an interface.

The 'traditional' software engineering approach generally begins by identifying the user requirements that comprise, for the most part, functional requirements. Obviously it is important to identify exactly what it is that a system is required to do, but very often the interface to a system is tacked on almost as an afterthought. In order to achieve a high level of usability, the interface designer must give early consideration to a number of important factors that are often neglected:

- the users;
- the context of use;
- the information architecture.

Section 1 outlined Abowd and Beale's (1991) General Interaction Framework. You will recall that there are four main components to this model: the input and output together forming the interface between the system and the user. Clearly, users need the facility to

17

input data with ease and to be able to make sense of data that is output from the system. Hence sensible design decisions have to be made in connection with choosing input and output methods that are appropriate for a particular user group and the context of use; additionally it is important to organise and output data so as to meet the user's information needs. There is not the space here to go into great depth about all these different topics, but this will serve as an introduction that will encourage you to conduct further research of your own.

CRUCIAL CONCEPT

The **scope** of interface design extends beyond what is seen on the screen; also, the different aspects that must be considered are interconnected.

The users and their characteristics

The first thing to consider is **who** will be using the system to ensure that your product fits their needs and abilities. As an interface designer you will need to analyse the target user population to answer such questions as:

- what personal characteristics shape their behaviour?
- what abilities do they have to perform the tasks required?
- are they enthusiastic learners?
- what prior experience do they have using similar products?
- what are their actual jobs/goals/tasks?

How does the interface designer go about answering some of these questions? There are numerous areas to investigate. For example, people all have different **cognitive** abilities – problem-solving, functional literacy, visual literacy, language ability, memory capacity/ function and so on. People also have different **physical** characteristics in terms of visual and auditory ability, they also vary in age and motor skills.

CRUCIAL TIP

Avoid making patronising assumptions about what people – especially the elderly or people with some sort of disability – can or can't do, **ask them.**

One of the main differences between groups of people is their ability (or lack of ability!) to use IT based products. It can sometimes be useful to categorise people as novice, intermediate or expert users and then incorporate features into a system that suit their general characteristics. Novice users are often afraid of looking stupid – especially in a work environment in front of their colleagues – and can be reluctant to explore in case of 'breaking something'. A system aimed at novice users should be designed in such a way that it is difficult to make errors, or if errors are made, that they can be recovered from easily. Intermediate users can be helped to learn how to use a new system by ensuring that it is consistent with a previous system (or another application in the same suite of programmes); in this way the users can build on their previous knowledge. Expert users could, for example, be provided with 'shortcuts' such as keystroke commands to replace mouse clicks – although these so called 'accelerators' are time-consuming to learn, expert users tend to enjoy finding out about them and find them quicker to use. Of course, some systems are targeted at a very general and diverse group of users. Most word-processing packages are used by a wide variety of people, so considerable skill is required to design this type of product and will probably involve numerous design trade-offs. Nevertheless, even in the case of a word-processor, one could assume perhaps (though not necessarily) a certain level of literacy amongst the users.

CRUCIAL CONCEPT

It is important to identify and analyse the **user characteristics** of the target user population to achieve a good 'fit' between the user and the system.

Context of use

In what context is the system you are designing going to be used? A ticket machine used by members of the public at a railway station is very different 'animal' from a browser used by an individual at home, and different again from an architectural design package used by a team of people working in separate locations. Preece *et al.* (2002) categorise context of use (sometimes referred to as environmental requirements) into four main aspects:

- **Physical environment** – e.g. is it likely to be noisy, bright, dark, crowded, dusty?
- **Social environment** – e.g. is the data being shared by people and if so, are these people co-located? Do users have to be able to work on data at the same time?
- **Organisational environment** – what kind of organisational culture exists? (For example, some organisations encourage employees to communicate informally, others frown on casual interactions). Is there likely to be training and other support provided? Do the users have to work with other media at the same time as using the system? (For example, referring to paper documents as well as looking at a screen.)
- **Technical environment** – what are the technical constraints? For example, an application may have to run on a particular operating system or be compatible with another application.

CRUCIAL CONCEPT

Identifying the **context of use** lends valuable insight into how people actually use a system in real situations, to do their work or for other purposes.

CRUCIAL TIP

Thinking about the user characteristics and the context of use can help the designer choose appropriate input/output methods. How long do you think a keyboard would last if was used for inputting requirements to a vending machine? And what percentage of the general public would know how to use a keyboard anyway?

Information architecture

Finally a brief mention of the concept of information architecture. What is information architecture? It depends who you ask, but in essence it is about organising, labelling and displaying data so that the user can navigate their way around a system and comprehend and make use of the information. It could be argued that data only becomes information when it has been carefully organised and presented. Information architecture is especially important when designing websites, but in my view the principles should be applied to all IT-based systems.

CRUCIAL TIP

Imagine going into a bookshop where all the volumes are just piled up in random heaps – it would be more or less impossible to find what you wanted. In fact, there is just such a bookshop in Brighton; it is said that the owner **can** actually find particular books in there. What are the implications of this anecdote for interface designers?

The interface designer (or more and more, specialist information architects) should therefore take care to:

- Group information into rational categories. Examples: on a website it would not make sense to put a company's telephone number on a different page from their postal address; a menu-based system needs to have similar options grouped together.
- Label categories appropriately. Examples: on a website, the links are often, effectively, labels – they (hopefully) inform the user what to expect; in the Microsoft Word

package, menu bar titles ('File' etc.) are labels, or headings, indicating what functions lie beneath.

- Present data (for example, text) so that it can be read easily. Examples: on a website, content needs to be organised in a different way from the same content published in a paper document; database output should be organised so that people can make use of it (rather than just outputting, say, the raw results of a query).

- In some situations it is necessary to index information, and there are many different indexing strategies to choose from. Examples: many websites provide an index to the content; help systems often index the topics.

CRUCIAL CONCEPT

Data only becomes information when it is grouped, labelled and presented effectively – this general idea is known as **information architecture**.

Quick test

1. What characteristics might small children and elderly people have in common?

2. Explain why a touchscreen would be a more appropriate input device than a keyboard for a railway ticket machine.

3. Imagine, on a company intranet, that the facility to book meeting rooms online is provided – in an index to this system, would you list it under 'M' for 'meeting rooms' or 'B' for 'booking'?

Section 4

User interface design – contributory disciplines

The design of effective interfaces incorporates skills and knowledge from many disciplines. This section outlines some of those disciplines and what they contribute to the theory and practice of interface design.

You are probably beginning to realise at this stage that an interface designer requires a range of skills beyond the ability just to write code. In fact it is possible to be a very effective designer and yet have very little in the way of programming skills – in large organisations, where software design is carried out by multi-disciplinary teams, the interface designer is often a specialist and would usually pass the final design to a programmer for implementation. *Some* knowledge of programming and how IT-based products work is obviously essential, but they are not the only skills required. Below, you will see a list of some of the disciplines that contribute to the understanding of interface design together with an idea of the kind of ideas that they contribute.

- **AI** – natural language research; problem solving; mental models; neural networks;
- **anthropolgy** – culture; differences in meaning of colour, music, symbols etc.;
- **cognitive psychology** – memory; perception; language understanding; problem-solving; mental models;
- **computer science** – software engineering; methodologies; hardware/software design;
- **design** – aesthetics; visual design; engineering design; affordance; visibility; graphics; typography;
- **ergonomics** – physical design of interface – input/output devices; screen resolution; safety etc.;

- **information architecture** – structure of information; labels; presentation;
- **information/library science** – organising/classifying/cataloguing/indexing information;
- **linguistics** – language acquisition and understanding; communication;
- **organisational psychology** – corporate culture; information flow; corporate structure; work practices; teams;
- **philosophy** – scientific approach to research; consciousness; ethics; logic; also linked to AI;
- **social psychology** – group behaviour; communication; decision making; CSCW (computer supported co-operative work);
- **sociology** – contextual design; ethnomethodology; linked to social psychology.

This rich array of disciplines underpinning what we know about HCI/interface design may appear very daunting, and nobody is suggesting that the interface designer is going to be an expert in all these fields. However, it is important for you have an awareness of some of these issues and perhaps an in-depth knowledge of one or two areas depending on your personal interests.

CRUCIAL CONCEPT

The study and practice of interface design is underpinned by a wide variety of disciplines.

Quick test

1. If you were in doubt about which method of indexing to use on, say, a commercial website, what type of professional could give some assistance with this?

2. Which area of research might you consult if you were designing a system that would be shared by many users?

Section 5

End of chapter assessment

Questions

1. Describe one model of human computer interaction (stating its source) and explain why it could be considered to be more complete than Norman's execution-evaluation cycle.

2. Why is the term 'usability' considered to be more rigorous than the term 'user friendly'?

3. Discuss some of the issues that would have to be taken into consideration when designing a passenger information system for a busy, main railway station.

4. Which discipline/s do you think it would be particularly important to take into account if you were designing a system with an international user base?

Approach to answers

1. Abowd and Beale's (1991) general interaction framework could be said to be more complete than Norman's execution-evaluation cycle since it incorporates a view of the system and not just the user. You would need to reproduce a version of Figure 1.1, and further, explain your diagram by describing the different components of the overall system and the steps in an interaction.

2. The term 'user friendly' could be considered to be imprecise and unquantifiable since it implies that a system is either 'friendly' or 'not friendly' on a simple bi-polar scale. By contrast, the term 'usability' has come to mean that a system can be assessed on a

whole range of criteria that are both specific and measurable. You could then go on to illustrate this idea by, for example, outlining Nielsen's (1993) usability attributes.

3. At the very least, one would have to consider:

- the users' characteristics – they would, for example, have a wide range of: ages; reading ability; visual and auditory acuity; physical ability; nationality etc.;
- context of use – noisy (how easy is it to hear announcements on platforms?); crowded; everyone in a hurry; people in different places etc.;
- information architecture – how to present a mass of information to people standing or moving about in different places? Screens showing final destinations? (Would everyone know that a train travelling to, for example Sidcup, would be the right one for Hither Green?) What colours should the text and background be – one big screen showing all the information or several small screens with information that scrolled (how quickly should it scroll?) etc.

4. Particular use would have to be made of research concerning anthropology, linguistics, sociology. This is because people from different cultures have different (learned) responses to sounds, music, colour, symbols and so on. As a very simple example, consider the differences between a (physical) US mailbox and a UK one and how they are represented in an email client. Is there a difference between a shopping 'cart' and a 'trolley'? Incidentally, do you think that all cultures understand the basic concept of a shopping trolley? (Not every country has the luxury of supermarkets.)

Section 6

Further reading and research

Further reading

Books and papers

Bias, R. G. and Mayhew, D. J. (Eds) (1994) – Chapter 3 (Clare-Marie Karat) 'A business case approach to usability cost justification'.

Dix, A. *et al.* (1998) – Chapter 3 'The interaction'.

Faulkner, X. (2000) – Chapter 2 'Usability – know the user!'.

Knight, J. and Jefsioutine, M. (2002).

Norman, D. A. (1998a) – it is hard to single out one particular part to recommend, it's well worth reading the whole book. This is a seminal, thought provoking publication.

Nielsen, J. (1993) – again it is worth reading the whole book at some stage, but you should at least read through Chapter 1 'Executive summary' and Chapter 2 'What is usability?'.

Preece, J. *et al.* (2002) – Chapter 1 'What is interaction design?'

Rosenfeld, L. and Morville, P. (1998) – Chapter 2 'Introduction to information architecture' and Chapter 3 'Organizing information'.

Websites

Bad Human Factors Designs. *http://www.baddesigns.com* (last accessed 24/11/02). A 'scrapbook of illustrated examples of things that are hard to use because they do not follow human factors principles.'

Isis Information Architects. *http://www.iarchitect.com* (last accessed 24/11/02). See especially, the 'interface hall of fame' and 'interface hall of shame' for numerous examples of good/poor quality interfaces together with enlightening explanations.

Further research

1. (a) In Section 1, an example was given of a hypothetical, unusable pen and paper-based writing system. Based on your own experience, think about some IT-based systems or software you have come across that is unusable in some respect. It's unlikely that anything will be as quite as poor as the exaggerated example, but think about and try to list the **specific** points that make the software in question awkward to use. Bear in mind what your actual aim is when using the software, for example, you may be trying to purchase an item from a website – are you actually able to fulfil this aim? If not, what has prevented you from doing it? How could it be made easier? How could it be made more pleasant to use?

   (b) In the same vein, identify a system that **is** usable in your opinion. Again, think about and list the particular aspects of it that make it easy to achieve your aims and enjoyable to use.

   (c) Write out five headings based on Nielsen's usability attributes. Then take all the points you identified in (a) and (b) above and try to categorise them under the appropriate heading. You may find that some of them fit under more than one heading, or that you require additional headings/attributes.

2. Get a group of, say, six people together around a table. If it is possible, put a large pile of fruit on the table (if this is not feasible, simply write down the names of as many fruits as you can think of on different pieces of paper). Now ask each person in turn to individually group the fruits into different categories and then label the categories. You may be surprised at the variety of ways in which people do this, for example some may group them by size, others by colour or by some other criteria. Think about the implications of this exercise when applied to the organisation and presentation of information via a computer system.

Chapter 2
Models of the user interface design process

Chapter summary

At present there is no one standard approach to designing user interfaces. This is because the field of user interface design has developed from many disciplines, each of which has contributed its own perspective and practices (see Chapter 1). Several different models of the process exist, each of which employs its own combination of design techniques. Specific design techniques are covered in Chapter 5.

This chapter introduces you to some of the key process models for creating user interface designs.

Learning outcomes

Outcome 1: The design lifecycle – understand the stages in the software lifecycle and where user interface design considerations fit in.

Outcome 2: Approaches to user interface design – identify different perspectives of user interface design.

Outcome 3: The development team – understand the roles within the software development team.

Outcome 4: Participative design (PD) – understand some specific user interface design models within the PD approach.
Question 1 at the end of the chapter tests you on this.

Outcome 5: User involvement – understand the advantages and difficulties of involving users in the user interface design process.
Question 2 at the end of the chapter tests you on this.

Outcome 6: Prototyping – understand the benefits and limitations of prototyping user interfaces.

How will you be assessed on this?

You will be expected to be aware of the relationship between user interface design and the wider software development process. This includes where user interface considerations fit in the software development life cycle, the different approaches to user interface design identified by Wallace and Anderson (1993) and the range and nature of roles within the software development team. You will need to explain certain approaches to user interface design within the participative design tradition and be able to describe and discuss the nature of prototyping user interfaces.

Section 1

The design lifecycle

The process of developing software can be regarded as a stage model. Certain activities happen at each stage and each stage has to be completed before the next can occur. A key consideration for user interface designers is where, in the overall software development process, the design of the user interface takes place.

A traditional model of systems development is the system lifecycle. There are many variants of this model, such as the Waterfall model (see Benyon, 1995), but a generic system lifecycle might look like this:

- requirements and function analysis;
- preliminary, high-level design;
- specification;
- design;
- testing and evaluation;
- production;
- maintenance.

CRUCIAL CONCEPT

The software development process is often considered to be **cyclical**: various activities take place in sequence. At the end of the process there is often a need for the product to be updated or more functionality to be added, so the cycle starts again.

At any stage, there might be a degree of iteration to the previous stage; and at the end of the cycle, there might be another complete cycle (a new version of the product is required, for instance).

CRUCIAL CONCEPT

Iteration, in this context, means going back a step in the cycle to deal with a problem that has come to light.

The point of interest from the perspective of interface designers is where in the cycle the design of the interface takes place.

Traditionally, the interface tended to be built towards the end of the cycle, when most of the functionality had been programmed in. There has been a growing awareness that more attention needs to be directed towards the design of the interface, especially since modern applications have a substantial proportion of the overall code supporting the interface; and because the majority of users are not experts. There now exist a number of approaches that explicitly address considerations of the design of the interface at points throughout the design lifecycle.

Quick test

1. Should the design of the user interface be left until the end of the software development process?

2. What does iteration mean?

Section 2

Approaches to interface design

This section looks at an influential paper by Wallace and Anderson (1993) that describes four discrete approaches to the design of user interfaces and suggests some characteristics that an ideal approach should possess.

Wallace and Anderson (1993) suggest that there are four identifiable approaches to user interface design:

- the craft approach;
- cognitive engineering;
- enhanced software engineering;
- the technologist approach.

The **craft approach** produces designs on the basis of the skill and experience of an expert designer who can be seen as a craftsman or artist. Each new design is unique and relies on the talent and creative abilities of the master designer. Design expertise is communicated by a process similar to that between a master craftsman and an apprentice: the apprentice learns by observation, imitation and practice. There is often no explicit process: the design is driven by the implicit knowledge of the expert.

This approach was common in the early days of user interface design and is still evident today, particularly with certain website designs. However, it tends to become inefficient once the problem domain becomes very complex and when changes in technologies occur. A good example of this was the development of graphical user interfaces in the middle 1980s: expert designers of command line interfaces were confronted with a transformation of the technology and much of their implicit knowledge was no longer applicable.

CRUCIAL CONCEPT

Craft approaches to user interface design tend to become inefficient when the design context changes or becomes very complex.

Cognitive engineering involves the application of cognitive psychological theory to user interface design. Cognitive psychology is broadly the study of how people think and, in particular, how they process information in order to guide action. Various models, such as the GOMS family of models (see Card, Moran and Newell, 1983) have been developed to predict how humans will interact with various alternative designs. The attraction of this approach is that applying these models to designs in their early stages (such as paper-based mock-ups) designers can identify optimum designs before embarking on the often time-consuming activity of producing fully functional applications (see Chapter 6 for a discussion of the use of predictive models in the evaluation of early designs). However, the early promise of cognitive engineering has not been widely fulfilled because it has proved time-consuming for most user interface designers to understand and learn to apply the models and also because the models themselves tend to have a very narrow scope of application.

Enhanced software engineering involves the introduction of HCI techniques into established software development methodologies. Structured design methods have not primarily been concerned with design of the user interface. Some successful attempts have been made to embed user interface techniques into, for example, SSADM and JSD (see Silcock *et al.*, 1990), in order to produce a specification for the user interface as well as for the underlying functional code. Again, however, the level of expertise required to carry out such analyses and the sheer complexity of the task has meant that, in practice, enhanced software engineering has not been widely adopted.

The **technologist approach** aims at automating the design process through the use of software tools, such as **user interface management systems** (**UIMS**). These tools support designers in specifying the layout or screen design, together with the dialogue between user and application.

Wallace and Anderson suggest that the aim of each of these approaches should be to improve the quality of both the completed design and the design process. They are all deficient in some respects, however, and the authors propose a set of 13 criteria for an effective design process. These include, for example:

- flexibility – any such approach should be adaptive to the needs of its users;
- communication – an ideal approach must enhance communication between those involved in the process;
- productivity – designer productivity must demonstrably improve;
- user participation – the process should support the participation of end users in the process;
- ease of use – the process should be easy to use and to learn;
- scope – the process should cover the whole of the product life cycle.

To date, no single user interface design process has been developed which incorporates all 13 criteria. Certain approaches within the participative design tradition address some of these criteria, particularly emphasising user involvement and communication between those involved in the process. Section 4 in this chapter covers participative design.

Quick test

1. What are the main weaknesses of the four approaches to user interface design described by Wallace and Anderson (1993)?

2. What characteristics should an ideal user interface design approach possess?

Section 3

The development team

This section looks at certain socio-organisational issues of product development teams, such as roles, responsibilities and structures. It also looks at problems that can arise and the arrangements that can be put in place to resolve them.

The design of user interfaces clearly cannot take place in isolation from the broader product development process. Some years ago it was not unknown for the user interface to be produced once the underlying application code had been developed: effectively an 'add-on'. It is now generally accepted that the user interface is too important to be regarded in this manner and that the development of the user interface must proceed in parallel with that of the functional software. In many applications nowadays the proportion of the code directly driving interaction with the user is greater than 50%.

This change in orientation has implications for the organisation of the product development team. Should it be organised as separate functional groups such as software engineers, user interface designers and usability testers; or as fully integrated, cross-functional groups? There is some evidence (e.g. Allen,1995; Hutchings and Knox,1995) that having different specialists working closely together in teams has significant benefits. Software engineers develop greater awareness of the importance of good user interface design and the requirements of end-users of their products, whilst usability specialists gain understanding of the software development process.

It is important that, within large application development projects where several designers may be contributing to the design of the user interface, strategic decisions are made by a single expert. This notion is advocated by authors such as Foley (1983) who suggests that a user interface architect take overall control for the structure and behaviour of the user interface. This view is echoed by Gugerty (1993) who uses the term 'superdesigner'. If such a role is not identified there is a real danger that the resulting product will be inconsistent in appearance and behaviour.

Whatever the particular organisational model adopted, problems and conflicts often arise within development teams due to misunderstandings, inadequate communication, internal politics etc. Whilst it is ultimately the responsibility of the manager of the team to resolve these problems, certain imperatives stand out. In the experience of the authors, it is especially important that:

- design decisions are clearly recorded and confirmed;
- responsibilities are firmly established;
- clear channels of communication are put in place.

A further imperative, emphasised by Kraut and Streeter (1995) is that the co-ordination of activities of team members is effectively managed. On large projects, particularly where there is a substantial degree of end-user involvement in the process, or when there is a significant degree of formative evaluation (see Chapter 6) and iterative design taking place, certain members of the design team may not be able to continue with their work until they receive inputs from others. This is not only inefficient but can be dangerous: rather than wait for the results of end-user feedback, designers may become impatient and produce further work along the wrong lines.

Quick test

1. What are the responsibilities of a user interface architect?

2. What kinds of problems can arise within development teams?

Section 4

Participative design

Participative design (PD) is a design philosophy that emphasises the importance of the end-users as key stakeholders in the software development process. Certain examples of PD models and processes are described and some problems of user involvement are discussed.

A prominent approach to product design in general and user interface design in particular is that of participative design (sometimes called participatory design). PD is a design philosophy or movement that arose in the Scandinavian countries and has become influential in Northern America and Western Europe in recent years. The central tenet of PD is that end-users of products are central actors in the development process. Most non-PD developmental approaches acknowledge user-involvement to some extent; in PD, how-ever, users are regarded as integral to the process.

CRUCIAL CONCEPT

User implies anyone who has some connection with the completed product. **End user** refers more specifically to those users who will use the product to a significant degree in their working lives.

PD embraces a range of developmental practices, methodologies, techniques and tools. It also incorporates many different models of how users participate in the development process.

Models of interaction between developers and users

For some development teams, the primary challenge is to acknowledge that the needs of users or customers should be taken seriously. A study by Allen (1995) describes the situation in a prominent software organisation where the products, although fully functional, were not being used by customers. Allen ascribes this to a culture prevailing within the team whereby the developers believed that they knew what was best for users and the emphasis was on writing elegant code rather than creating usable products. Allen describes how he, as the newly appointed manager of this team managed, over time, to establish a customer-centred paradigm within the team.

CRUCIAL CONCEPT

Paradigm – in this context a framework or mind-set – is where the needs of customers come first.

Other models emphasise more strongly the need for more direct user participation in the development process. **Joint application development (JAD)** is now a well-established method where users participate in design teams (see e.g. Bødker,1996).

Contextual design (Beyer and Holzblatt, 1995) differs from JAD in that the designers do a significant amount of their work in the end-users' own environments. A project starts by the designers talking to and observing end-users as they do their everyday work. The data that emerge from these sessions is then interpreted within cross-functional teams so that all involved can gain a shared perspective on the users' world. Solutions are progressively and iteratively developed using storyboards and paper-based mock-ups, until the final design is agreed upon in the form of an object model. Only then does the software implementation begin.

User-centred design approaches

PD approaches have started to influence the software development practices of a number of prominent organisations. Several companies have produced their own proprietary design approaches, based on the notion of the centrality of the end-user in the process. Some examples include:

- IBM's UCD (Vredenburg, 1999)
- Bang and Olufsen (Bærentsen and Slavensky, 1999)
- Kommunedata (KMD) (Gardner, 1999)
- Microsoft (Muller and Czerwinski, 1999)

As an illustration of these user-centred approaches, the **user-involvement method (UIM)** (see Axtell et al.,1997) is here outlined in Figure 2.1. This method was developed in a large UK-based organisation in order to help with the design and development of a substantial software application to support the administrative activities of a large number of staff. Following a lengthy requirements analysis phase a user group was established, which consisted of four or five representative users. Alongside the user group was a cooperative of one user and a developer.

On the basis of information in the requirements analysis, the cooperative first undertook a task analysis (see Chapter 5 for a description of task analysis). The accuracy of the task analysis was checked with the user group. The cooperative then produced prototype screen designs, which were also given to the user group for their comment and feedback.

In this way, aspects of the design could be successively built up, refined and validated. This iterative cycle of design and feedback continued until the evolving design was sufficiently stable to be implemented.

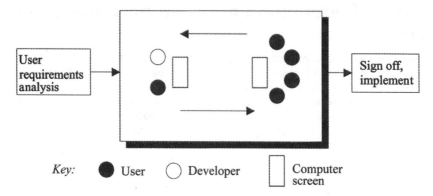

Figure 2.1 Illustration of UIM (after Axtell et al., 1997)

Who are the users?

A key issue in PD-influenced methodologies is who actually are the users of the product. This might seem a perverse question and clearly the answer is that, ideally, those end users who will actually use the product must be involved with the development team. Instead, in many cases, there is a marked tendency for intermediaries or surrogates to take the role of end users, e.g.

- marketing people;
- systems analysts;
- supervisors etc.

Keil and Carmel (1995) report an investigation of 14 software development projects, half of which were regarded as successful whilst the remainder failed in some respects to achieve their aims. In particular, the authors studied the types of links (communication channels) between developers and users within each of these projects. Links included, for example, JAD workshops, focus groups and exposure of users to prototypes. The findings were that the successful projects had used **more links** and, significantly, **more direct links** than unsuccessful projects. By direct links, the authors mean that designers were able to interact directly with the end-users rather than relying on intermediaries (such as supervisors, middle managers) to communicate requirements.

Participative design techniques

PD is both eclectic and pragmatic in its adoption and use of techniques. Muller et al. (1993) provide a useful classification of commonly used techniques, based on the point in the development process they are most appropriately used, and whether the emphasis is on the user entering the designers' world or vice versa.

--- CRUCIAL TIP ---

PD is eclectic in the sense that techniques are taken from a range of different disciplines and pragmatic because the focus is on practicality and efficiency.

Is user involvement always beneficial?

PD methodologies clearly meet several of Wallace and Anderson's criteria for an ideal process (see Section 2 in this chapter) such as a high degree of user-involvement in the process, but does it meet them all? A study by Heinbokel *et al.* (1996) suggests that there are problems with user involvement in the development process. For example this particular study demonstrated that user participation led to:

- low overall success of the project;
- few design innovations;
- high stress in the team.

The study by Axtell *et al.* (1997), outlined above, revealed problems with the particular model of user-involvement adopted (UIM), such as:

- too much repetition of work, confusion over decisions;
- time for design decisions to be taken was too long;
- users don't possess sufficient knowledge to contribute significantly;
- users require significant training.

It is, of course, unrealistic to assume that, by bringing end-users to the centre of the product development process, all problems will be automatically resolved. Large-scale software development is an extraordinarily complex undertaking, requiring high levels of technical and managerial competence in a context of changing organisational and human requirements. The issue remains, however, that if end-users are ignored or marginalised in the process, there are very real risks that software products will be underused or rejected by the very people for whom they have been designed.

A study by Damodaran (1996) discusses some of the problems associated with user involvement. One interesting phenomenon that she discusses is the tendency of some users involved with the design team to become 'hostages'. Because of their relative lack of technical knowledge such users tend to go along with decisions made by the designers in order to keep the peace. Consequently design decisions are unchallenged and user-involvement is illusory.

Damodaran provides practical advice regarding such issues as identifying the range of user roles (top management, middle management and end-users), the training needs of users and how the process of user involvement should be managed.

Quick test

1. What are the benefits and problems associated with a high degree of user-involvement?
2. What evidence is there that direct links between developers and end-users result in more successful projects?

Section 5

Prototyping

In this section, the use of **prototyping** as a means of creating user interfaces is presented. Various categories of prototypes are outlined and their advantages and limitations are discussed.

Prototyping is the activity of creating partial designs, quickly and at low cost, in order to allow designers to get feedback from users at an early stage of the design process. It can also be used to create several alternative designs which can be compared or evaluated using one or more **formative techniques** (see Chapter 6). Prototyping is commonly used within the participative design tradition. Its benefits are widely accepted but there is no single, standardised process.

The prototyping process

Although there are many variations in the practice of prototyping, the following is a summary of the generic process:

(a) **identify initial user requirements** using techniques such as focus groups, stakeholder analysis etc.;
(b) **develop a prototype** using appropriate screen layout, dialogue design and navigational guidelines;
(c) **use and evaluate the prototype** with the aid of user tests, walkthroughs etc.;
(d) **revise the prototype** using the evaluation results;
(e) **go to** (c).

How many times it is necessary to go around the loop between (c) and (e) depends on a number of factors such as how quickly usability faults are discovered and how much time is available.

Types of prototypes

There are several different species of prototypes. Rettig (1994) makes the distinction between 'hi-tech' and 'low-tech' while other practitioners (e.g. Greenberg, 1998) use a categorisation of:

- low-fidelity;
- medium-fidelity;
- high-fidelity prototypes.

Broadly, low-tech or low-fidelity prototyping involves the creation of paper-based sketches or mock-ups to represent the appearance and behaviour of the user interface. High-fidelity prototypes are substantially complete computer-based applications, which allow users to interact with much of the functionality of the final product. Medium-fidelity prototypes typically are computer-based simulations, which may not be fully interactive and which allow access to only a small degree of functionality.

CRUCIAL CONCEPT

The **fidelity** of prototypes refers to the extent to which the prototype design accurately reflects the appearance (e.g. the screen layout) and behaviour of the application.

Another distinction that is made is between horizontal and vertical prototypes (see Rudd *et al.*, 1996). Vertical prototypes are high-fidelity prototypes which, however, represent only a proportion of the intended functionality of the final product. Horizontal prototypes model the complete range of user interaction at a surface level but do not provide access to the detailed, lower-level functionality.

Low-fidelity prototypes

Various paper-based tools are used to mock-up sketches, scenarios and storyboards (see Chapter 5 for a description of these design techniques). These tools can range from hand-drawn representations of screen layouts on paper to more elaborate models created from kits of user interface components, such as cardboard buttons, menu bars, dialogue boxes, scroll bars etc.

Once the prototype has been created, users are encouraged to interact with it. Rettig (1994) describes a process for obtaining quick feedback from users using low-tech prototypes. One member of the design team acts as a facilitator, giving users instructions and advice while another team member acts as the 'computer', implementing the consequences of user actions by manipulating the user interface components in response to user actions. Other team members videotape the session or take notes. At the end of the session, the team discusses the findings and any changes to the prototype can be easily made.

Medium- and high-fidelity prototypes

There exists a range of software prototyping tools, such as HyperCard, Microsoft PowerPoint and Microsoft Visual Basic, which permit partial or fully functional prototypes to be relatively quickly and easily created. Users can interact more naturally with computer-based than with paper-based prototypes: selection of an icon, for example, will cause the appropriate function to be fired or, at least, simulated.

The higher the fidelity of the prototype, the more realistic it will appear to users. In particular, it is easier to design and test the dynamic (i.e. navigational) aspects of the user interface using computer-based prototypes rather than paper-based ones.

Selection of prototyping approaches

Low-fidelity prototyping is generally regarded as a quick and low-cost activity that provides useful feedback about the overall design concept and static (i.e. screen layout) aspects of the user interface design. Higher-fidelity prototypes tend to take longer to develop and require a degree of expertise in using a software prototyping tool. The selection of which approach to take depends on a range of factors, such as:

- the size and scope of the intended application;
- time frame for development;
- expertise available.

In many large-scale projects the issue is not simply whether to use a low-fidelity or medium-fidelity prototyping approach but rather how to plan and integrate the overall development process. A pragmatic or evolutionary approach might be to:

- carry out an initial user requirements analysis;
- produce an initial low-fidelity, paper-based prototype in order to explore the main design concepts and screen layout issues;
- build a medium-fidelity prototype, perhaps a simulation;
- produce a number of vertical, high-fidelity prototypes;
- integrate the vertical prototypes into a complete, fully-functional high fidelity prototype.

Each of these stages is influenced by user feedback and evaluation of the prototype.

In some instances the final prototype may be, effectively, the finished product. In general, however, the prototype is used as one of a number of specification instruments for the software developers, since the overall application may need to be built using a software environment more powerful than that of a quick prototyping tool.

In summary, prototyping can be used by designers and users who are well informed about its benefits and limitations. The process must not be haphazard but must be planned, with explicit version and documentation controls. Most importantly, the organisational climate must be supportive to the concepts of user involvement and cycles of iterative design and evaluation (see Alavi, 1984).

Quick test

1. How is low-fidelity prototyping carried out?

2. What are the main advantages and limitations of medium-fidelity prototyping?

Section 6

End of chapter assessment

Questions

1. The participative design (PD) tradition emphasises the centrality of end-users within the user interface design process. Describe any one PD technique that is based on significant end-user involvement.

2. Discuss both the advantages and problems of involving users in the user interface design process, drawing upon evidence from the academic literature.

3. Describe and discuss the nature of prototyping user interfaces.

Approach to answers

1. There are several possibilities here, such as contextual inquiry, various prototyping approaches, the user-involvement method (Axtell *et al.*, 1997) etc. Marks will be given on the bases of the accuracy and completeness of the description.

2. Advantages: ensures user-commitment to the finished product; increased job satisfaction, sense of ownership of design on the part of users; evidence that user involvement results in better (both more usable and more appropriately functional) products (Keil and Carmel, 1995).

   Problems: can stifle designer creativity, lengthen project time; users need training (Axtell *et al.*, 1997). Some users can become 'hostages' to the design team (Damodaran, 1996); selecting appropriate users, rather than surrogates and intermediaries.

3. Identifying user requirements, using appropriate techniques, such as focus groups; developing the prototype with the aid of relevant guidelines; using and evaluating the prototype; and revising the prototype, drawing on the results of evaluation studies.
   The discussion should emphasise the iterative nature of prototyping and point out that there exist several 'species' of prototypes, such as low- and high-fidelity.

Section 7

Further reading and research

Further reading

Books and papers
Beyer, H. and Holztblatt, K. (1998) – Chapter 3 'Principles of contextual enquiry'.
Rettig (1994).
Dix, A. *et al.* (1998) – Section 5.5 'Iterative design and prototyping'.
Madsen (1999).
Norman, D. A. (1998b) – Chapter 9 'Human-centered development'.
Torres, R. J. (2002) – Chapter 4 'A user-centred product team'.
Vredenburg (1999).

Websites

InContext. *http://www.incent.com/cd/cdhow.html* InContext is a US-based usability consultancy founded by Karen Holtzblatt and Hugh Beyer. This link gives an interesting description of the processes involved in contextual design.

Prototyping for Design and Evaluation. *http://pages.cpsc.ucalgary.ca/~saul/681/1998/prototyping/survey.html* A comprehensive review of prototyping techniques written by Professor Saul Greenberg, University of Calgary.

SERCO. *http://www.usability.serco.com/services/services.htm* An overview of the services offered by SERCO, a large UK usability consultancy; it outlines the processes involved in user-centred system design.

Further research

1. Plan an exercise to create a paper prototype of a PDA (personal digital assistant). You will need to consider the functionality that will be modelled, the materials you will use and the time scales. It will be necessary to consider the extent of user-involvement in the process, for example the number of users, how representative they are and what activities they are required to undertake.

2. You will probably have to undertake further research in order to produce your plan effectively. When you are satisfied with your plan, carry out the prototyping activity. When the exercise is complete, review the effectiveness of the process with regard to (in particular) the efficacy of the paper-based materials you have used and the advantages and problems associated with involving the users.

Chapter 3
Design guidance: principles, guidelines and standards

Chapter summary

There is a wealth of guidance available to support the design of user interfaces. This chapter will help you to realise the benefits of deploying guidelines in all their forms, enable you to distinguish between the different types, and take account of some of the practical issues inherent in deploying guidelines.

Learning outcomes

Outcome 1: Demonstrate an awareness of the benefits associated with the use of design guidance.
There are measurable benefits to be obtained by designers, end-users and organisations from utilising design guidance. Question 1 at the end of the chapter tests your awareness of these benefits.

Outcome 2: Demonstrate an understanding of the characteristics of different types of design guidance and the relationship between them.
You will need to be able to distinguish between the various forms and characteristics of design guidelines and understand their relationship. Question 2 at the end of the chapter assesses your ability to do this.

Outcome 3: Discuss the issues involved in the practical use of design guidelines.
Question 3 at the end of the chapter gives you the opportunity to do this.

How will you be assessed on this?

In an examination, you may be asked to discuss the benefits and problems associated with the use of design guidance. You would be expected to understand the difference between the different types of guidance, explain their characteristics and relationships and be familiar with the main types of standards. Answers would benefit from using specific published examples. You might be asked to discuss the relative merits of using/not using particular guidelines or explain why there is sometimes resistance to using them and so on. In general, you would need to be able to present arguments for and against certain ideas and explain why you personally favour one approach over another – you would need to support your arguments by citing from the literature in order to get higher marks.

In your practical work, you would be expected to identify and make use of appropriate design guidance. Your choice of guidelines should be supported by a rationale for that decision and you should be able to explain **how** they were used. A reflective approach should be demonstrated, i.e. you should be able to discuss rationally how using these guidelines actually worked in practice and what lessons had been learned.

Section 1

Why make use of guidelines?

It is important to understand the positive contribution that design guidance in all its forms can make to the design of IT systems in general, and user interfaces in particular. Identifying and deploying appropriate guidelines help to design interfaces with a high degree of usability – guidelines assist designers so that users and organisations can benefit from usable IT systems.

CRUCIAL TIP

In this chapter and elsewhere in the book, the term **guidelines** is sometimes used in a generic sense, i.e. as a general term for all kind of design guidance that encompasses principles and standards as well as guidelines *per se*. By the end of this chapter you will be able to distinguish where 'guidelines' is being used generically or in the more specific meaning of the term.

Reed *et al.* (1999) point out that published standards and guidelines for user interfaces have increased in importance since the mid 1980s, which is when the use of computers started to become pervasive, particularly in work environments. In their view, there are substantial benefits to be accrued from using guidelines to inform the design of user interfaces for example:

- increased productivity;
- reduced physical and mental stress;
- reduced training costs;
- improvements in user-system interoperability across applications;
- improved overall product quality including aesthetics.

Some of these issues should be familiar to you from Chapter 1 which is where the idea was introduced that usable systems give rise to tangible and measurable benefits both to the individual user and to the organisation they work for. It is clear then that the various attributes of usability – for example, efficiency and memorability – are general design principles that should be aimed for. On a practical level, the use of guidelines can:

- ensure a degree of consistency within and between designs;
- reduce the likelihood of significant design flaws;
- form the basis of future standardisation activities, i.e. designers don't have to 'reinvent the wheel' every time a new design activity is commenced.

Newman and Lamming (1995) identify four main roles for guidelines to enhance the design process:

- raising awareness – e.g. by introducing concepts which the designer may not be aware of, such as methods of displaying windows etc.;
- assisting in choices – for example should the 'home' link on a web page be at the top, the bottom or somewhere else?;
- offering strategies – general strategies may already exist to assist with solving a particular design problem, for example displaying a large number of choices in menus could be achieved by using cascading menus;
- supporting evaluation – guidelines can be used as a checklist for reviewing the design to measure the extent to which it meets certain criteria.

CRUCIAL CONCEPT

Guidelines have a variety of different uses – raising awareness; assisting in choices; offering strategies; supporting evaluation.

Guidelines (in the general sense of the term) can be thought of as rules that should be followed in the design process so as to maximise the usability of a product. Dix *et al.* (1998) usefully classify these rules along two dimensions: authority and generality. By authority, Dix *et al.* mean whether or not a rule should be followed rigidly or whether it is more of a suggestion or hint. Generality is an indication of whether a rule is widely applicable to any interface design endeavour or whether it is more narrowly applicable. Standards, for example, tend to be high in terms of authority and limited as to their application whereas guidelines are usually low in authority and general in application. Figure 3.1 below illustrates this idea.

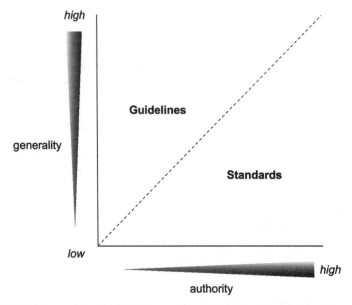

Figure 3.1 Guidelines and standards in terms of generality and authority. After Dix et al. (1998)

CRUCIAL CONCEPT

Amongst other things, the use of **design guidelines** helps the designer to maximise usability and ensure consistency. Guidelines vary in their degree of generality and authority.

In the next section we will be looking in more detail at principles, guidelines and standards. For now, you need to understand that effective user interface design is supported by standards and guidelines that, in turn, are underpinned by theoretical principles. Figure 3.2 below gives an idea of this concept.

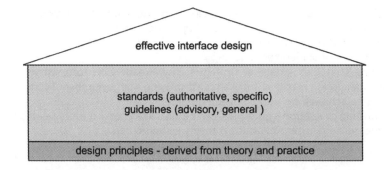

Figure 3.2 The characteristics of and relationship between principles, guidelines and standards

On the face of it then, the use of guidelines is a 'good thing' – however as you will come to recognise, there can be problems and limitations as well as benefits associated with their use.

Quick test

1. In what ways are guidelines and standards characterised?

2. Outline the main uses of guidelines.

Section 2

Principles, guidelines and standards

There are many different forms of design support available. These range from generic principles and guidelines through to legal standards. In this section you will learn to recognise the differences and relationships between the various types of design guidance available and start to think about finding sources of guidance, making distinctions between these sources and choosing the most appropriate for the design task in hand.

Design principles

Design principles have a number of characteristics – they tend to be very high level in that they are quite general and could be applied to a wide range of software products. They can derive from empirical research or from experience, and many academics and design practitioners have devised various sets of principles. The tables below illustrate two well known examples.

Nielsen and Molich's (1990) heuristics (Table 3.1) are primarily intended as an evaluation tool for use by usability evaluators, in effect a checklist, however they can also be viewed as a set of high level principles to guide designers. You will see that they are clearly understandable without explanation. Or are they? One of the problems with general principles is the question of interpretation, for example the programmer might consider that a system is consistent whereas the user could disagree.

Table 3.1 Nielsen and Molich's (1990) heuristics for design evaluation

Be consistent	Provide short cuts
Provide feedback	Provide good error messages
Provide clearly marked exits	Minimise the user's memory load
Use simple and natural dialogue	Speak the user's language
Prevent errors	

CRUCIAL CONCEPT

A **heuristic** in this context, can be thought of as a common sense 'rule of thumb'.

Dix *et al.* (1998) have taken the approach of categorising usability principles under three main headings: learnability, flexibility and robustness. Each of these main categories is sub-divided into more specific principles, thus creating an extensible taxonomy. Learnability refers to the ease with which a new user can familiarise themselves with a system and use it effectively. There are multiple ways in which the user and a system can interact, this is covered by the main principle of flexibility. Robustness covers the provision of effective levels of support to the user. Again, we may have the challenge of interpreting consistently the exact meaning of these high level principles in practice.

Table 3.2 Dix *et al.* (1998) principles to support usability

Learnability	Flexibility	Robustness
Predicatability	Dialogue initiative	Observability
Synthesisability	Multi-threading	Recoverability
Familiarity	Task migratability	Responsiveness
Generalisability	Substitutivity	Task performance
Consistency	Customisability	

You will see from Tables 3.1 and 3.2 that there are some principles in common, for example 'consistency' (incidentally, consistency probably features in virtually all sets of design principles) – illustrating how principles tend to be fairly general in their nature. In essence, then, design principles help the designer to understand what they should be aiming for in terms of the characteristics a system should have in order to be usable. What principles don't do is explain **how** to achieve these desirable usability attributes, which is where usability guidelines and standards come in.

CRUCIAL CONCEPT

Design principles tend to be high level (widely applicable and general); derive from theory and practice; underpin guidelines and standards.

Usability guidelines

Usability guidelines can take many forms such as checklists, style guides, hints, tips, recommendations and so on, so you may come across a variety of different terms. Guidelines tend to be advisory in nature and, although they **can** be more specific than principles, they tend to lack the authority and specificity afforded by standards. In common with principles and standards they can derive from empirical research or from practitioner experience, however there is a view that the most valid and reliable guidelines emanate from sound research and theoretical principles.

CRUCIAL TIP

The terms **valid** and **reliable** have a specific meaning in the general field of data measurement/collection/ analysis. In the context of usability, validity could mean ensuring that you are **actually** measuring the attribute you **think** you are measuring. For example: you follow particular guidelines to ensure, say, learnability. Evaluation confirms that the system does indeed adhere to the guidelines – but how confident can you be that the guidelines do in fact measure the extent of **learnability**? Reliability essentially refers to the consistency of results. See Hughes (1999) for more information.

Gardiner and Christie (1987) furnish a good example of how guidelines are derived from a theoretical base. In the context of cognitive psychology theory, academic researchers identified 85 cognitive principles of relevance to interface design. The principles were then grouped into 14 dimensions, for example 'navigation', 'error management' etc. The principles were then translated by design practitioners into an extensive set of guidelines with practical application. This approach exemplifies a rational approach to the production of guidelines; additionally it demonstrates how researchers and practitioners can combine their specialist skills and knowledge to transfer academic theory to the commercial domain. You may also recall, from Chapter 1, how a whole range of disciplines contribute to the study and practice of interface design.

Another example from Gerhardt-Powals (1996) uses empirical research to lend support to the hypothesis that a cognitively engineered interface is more effective (in this context – enhances user performance, reduces work load and increases user satisfaction) than an interface that is not cognitively engineered. The experiment utilised a decision-support system for an anti-submarine warfare (ASW) application. Ten cognitive principles were identified from the literature, such as 'automate unwanted workload', 'reduce uncertainty' and so on. The cognitive principles were then applied to one of three versions of the decision-support system and each of the three versions of the system was subjected to evaluation. The results were interpreted as supporting the hypothesis, i.e. the cognitively engineered interface was more effective than the other two. Interestingly, in this example, some application of the cognitive principles appears to contradict other accepted principles, in particular the use of colour coding. For example, the principle 'automate unwanted workload' was implemented by colouring the display of critical parameters such as dive angles as either green (safe) or red (unsafe). There exists a generally accepted principal that the use of green and red colours to impart important information should be avoided in an interface because of the possibility of confusion by persons who have colour deficient vision (Preece et al. 1994). This particular principle derives from extensive research which shows that most people have three classes of cone receptors in the retina – implicated in colour perception – but some have only two or one (Kaiser, 2002). One can only hope that the users of the ASW system are not colour deficient!

It can be seen that, whereas principles can be thought of as characteristics to aim for, guidelines (in their various roles) offer support to the designer in terms of **how** to achieve adherence to particular principles. Table 3.3, below, gives an indication of how hypothetical guidelines relate to particular principles.

Table 3.3 Principles and associated guidelines

Principle	Guideline
Consistency	Always place home button at top left hand corner
Recoverability	Always provide an undo function
Feedback	Always provide a progress bar to indicate degree of process completeness
Flexibility	Always provide keyboard accelerators as an alternative to using the mouse

You will, I hope, notice that the guidelines shown in Table 3.3 are still quite vague. For example 'Always place home button at top left-hand corner' says nothing about other attributes of the button such as its size or colour. This is a characteristic of many sets of guidelines, which you will recall from earlier in this chapter tend to be quite general in nature. It is worth noting however, that some sets of guidelines are much more explicit, and yet others pertain to particular types of systems, for example Maguire's (1999) review of user-interface design guidelines for public information kiosks. Next we will be examining the type of guidelines that tend to be more specific and authoritative – standards.

─────────── CRUCIAL CONCEPT ───────────

Usability guidelines offer support to the designer to achieve adherence to particular design principles. They vary in terms of their generality, but in the main they tend to the generic and are advisory as opposed to authoritative in nature.

Usability standards

Standards are prescribed ways of presenting, doing or communicating something to achieve a measure of consistency. As a simple example from everyday life, consider traffic lights – it is not hard to imagine the chaos that would ensue if each local authority chose to deploy different coloured lights instead of the familiar red, yellow and green. There are many reasons why applying standards to interface design is also a valuable activity; for example Stewart (1999) considers that usability standards are important in terms of: achieving consistency; maintaining good practice; promoting common understanding between users, suppliers and regulators; fulfilling legal obligations; prioritising user interface issues.

There exist several different types of standards relating to IT that differ in terms of their authority and scope, in other words they have different status. IT standards may be categorised in the following way:

- **in-house** – e.g. style guides/checklists and so on to guide the production of, for example, a company intranet;

- **proprietary** – developed and established by one particular manufacturer, e.g. Microsoft Windows;

- *de facto* – generally accepted and adhered to, but with no formal status, often associated with economically successful products, e.g. again, Microsoft Windows;

- *de jure* – formal, usually agreed by consensus between interested parties, legal status. Various national and international organisations establish and maintain *de jure* standards such as the International Organisation for Standardisation, the National Physical Laboratory in the UK, the National Institute of Standards and Technology in the USA, the European Computer Manufacturers Association.

This list can be extended by adding a relatively recent category – **open source**. The criteria for open source software comprises: free distribution, inclusion of the source code and allowing modification to that code. The Linux operating system is a typical instance of open source software.

You may recall from Chapter 1 the definition of usability as set out in ISO 9241-11: Guidance on Usability, 1998. It may surprise you to know that there are numerous other ISO standards that relate to interface design and usability. TRUMP (Trial Usability Maturity Principles – a project part funded by the European Commission under ESPRIT project 28015) categorises usability standards thus:

1. the use of the product (effectiveness, efficiency and satisfaction in a particular context of use);
2. the user interface and interaction;
3. the process used to develop the product;
4. the capability of an organisation to apply user centred design.

There is not the scope here to list or describe in detail all the usability related standards but it is worth having a very brief look at the main features of two of them:

ISO 9241-11: Guidance on Usability – which fits into category 1 in the TRUMP scheme – defines the usability of the whole system. It centres on three main factors: effectiveness, efficiency and satisfaction. The point about these factors is that they can be evaluated using measurable criteria, for example the minimum time to complete a task.

ISO 13407: Human-centred Design Processes for Interactive Systems – which fits into category 3 in the TRUMP scheme – provides guidance on human-centred design activities throughout the life cycle of interactive computer-based systems. It covers hardware and software, promotes human factors and ergonomics, gives guidance for project managers and is complementary to ISO 9241. Question 2 at the end of this chapter provides the opportunity for you to find out more about ISO 13407 and to think about how it could be used in practice; Chapter 4 outlines the general framework in further detail.

The previous sections have focused on identifying the characteristics of the various types of guidelines and some of the benefits associated with their use. In the next section we will discuss some of the potential problems associated with their use in practice.

> ──────── CRUCIAL CONCEPT ────────
>
> There are many sets of **standards**, with different status, associated with IT in general and interface design and usability in particular. Usability related standards can be categorised according to their main purpose.

Quick test

1. List as many design principles as you can remember from your reading so far.

2. Describe how usability guidelines can be derived.

3. Outline two important usability related standards and say where they fit into the TRUMP scheme.

Section 3

Challenges associated with using guidelines

Understanding the benefits of deploying design guidance and understanding the various forms available are only part of the interface design process. This chapter draws your attention to some of the practical issues involved in selecting and applying appropriate guidelines.

The first challenge lies in selecting guidelines that are appropriate for the particular task in hand. At the simplest level, there would be little point in, for instance, using a set of web design guidelines to inform the design of a public information kiosk in a museum – this would be an example of particular guidelines being **too** specific and out of context. At the other end of the scale, as we saw in the previous section, some guidelines are, by contrast, extremely general, for example 'always provide feedback' could be interpreted in a number of ways. We also saw in the previous section (the ASW system) how the interpretation of a principle contradicted another principle, so clearly the designer is often faced with making some sort of design trade-off.

> ──────── CRUCIAL TIP ────────
>
> A **trade-off** is where a design decision, say, in terms of a certain feature, is made at the expense of another feature. In the ASW example the designers may, for example, have decided that it was better to implement the display of critical parameters in red and green colours for clarity. Perhaps the assumption was that the operators of these sorts of systems would have been screened for colour blindness.
> It is always a good idea to document design trade-offs for future reference.

Then there are questions relating to derivation – what is the provenance of a set of guidelines, is there some evidence as to the extent of their validity and reliability? One would have more confidence in guidance that had emanated from properly conducted research than from a pundit merely expressing an opinion.

> ──────── CRUCIAL CONCEPT ────────
>
> **Guidelines** in practical use can be too general or too specific, they may be ambiguous in which case there can be variance in their interpretation. Different sets of guidelines may be contradictory. The derivation of some guidelines is dubious.

Interface designers can be reluctant to use guidelines for diverse reasons. There is evidence (Löwgren and Laurén 1993) to suggest that guidelines are hard to use in terms of:

- **accessibility** – they may be hard to locate, be poorly organised, badly written and so on;

- **interpretation** – we have already noted that many guidelines, especially if they tend to the generic, can be interpreted in a variety of ways;

- **contextualisation** – on one level, this is simply to do with using the most appropriate guidance for the design problem. In another sense, it concerns the presentation and filtering of guidance information in such a way that its relevance and meaning are obvious.

Löwgren and Laurén conducted an experiment with interface designers to see how they made use of a style guide relating to the use of Motif (a Unix GUI standard) while designing an interface prototype. The research was conducted to inform the requirements for a design-support tool. It was observed that the designers approached the guidelines in different ways and employed different tactics and reading styles – one, for example, used them frequently on a daily basis, another skimmed through them and never referred to them again, others did not consult them at all. Deviations from the style guide requirements were analysed and the designers were interviewed to try to establish why the deviations were made. Two important findings emerged which were, first, that the designers needed to feel in control of support such as the proposed design-support tool and secondly that they wanted some indication of the degree of any violation from the guidelines – was it, for example, a deviation from Motif standards or merely a deviation from a general design principle? The implication of this, and similar research, is that design guidance must itself be made usable in order to offer any real utility to interface designers and that designers should not feel that their creativity and innovation are compromised. There is also a connection here with providing guidance and support to end users, which will be covered in Chapter 8.

CRUCIAL CONCEPT

Design guidance is often considered to be difficult to use. Design guidelines in all their forms must be accessible and their precise meaning and context should be clear. Designers must feel that **they** are in control of their work and that their creativity and innovation is not constrained.

To what extent do guidelines **actually** ensure usability? From what you've been reading in this section up to now, some of you might get the impression that, providing the 'right' set of guidelines are chosen and applied in the 'correct' way, the designer will end up creating a usable system. Unfortunately, the process of effective design is not that simple – or perhaps fortunately, since the challenge of solving tricky design problems is what makes it so interesting. Buie (1999) considers that, in particular, general guidelines cannot address:

- a specific user population in a particular context of work;
- constraints and issues imposed by the context;
- the structure and content of the information exchanged during the interactions between the user and the system.

These are what Buie accurately describes as the 'hard parts of HCI design'. To cover these 'hard parts' she suggests that in addition to using standards which prescribe, for example, how objects should be aligned on the screen, that an 'HCI **process**' (emphasis added) is required. Cast your mind back to ISO 13407 outlined in the previous section – this is specifically a **process** standard, so presumably, it would cover this concern. The caveat that Buie – and others – apply to ISO 13407 is that this standard is viewed as being very general, and that it should be tailored to an individual organisation's requirements. I must add here that, in my view, the beauty of ISO 13407 is precisely the reason that some appear to treat it with some caution, i.e. it is **advisory** and provides a framework to support the design process rather than a straightjacket to constrain it. One size cannot realistically fit all.

Another criticism sometimes levied at IT standards relates to the fact that the IT industry is very fast-moving and that the somewhat long-winded process of developing standards lags behind innovation. Other critics point to the relative formality and apparently restrictive nature of standards. People like Tom Stewart who are heavily involved in the development of standards acknowledge these, and other negative reactions. Stewart (2000), however, counters some of these comments by pointing out that:

- relatively slow development of standards ensures maximum consultation; avoids the premature publication of standards (ensuring current relevance); allows those who may be affected (e.g. hardware and software producers) more time to prepare to meet the standard;

- formal standards can be included in procurement processes to, for example, demonstrate good practice;

- the various parts of ISO 13407, in particular, often contain only one 'shall' – generally to prescribe the nature of evidence required to show that relevant recommendations in the standard have been followed.

CRUCIAL CONCEPT

The general idea of **formal standards** is accepted, but they are criticised by some for either being too formal or not formal enough – there are supporters and detractors for each point of view. Others hold the view that standards are too slow in development and that they are restrictive – again, there are arguments for and against these allegations.

Quick test

1. What are some of the criticisms of guidelines in general, and standards in particular?
2. What are the main points to consider when producing guidance for designers?

Section 4

End of chapter assessment

Questions

1. Outline the benefits of using design guidance.
2. Explain the meaning of, and differentiate between, design principles, usability guidelines and standards, illustrating your answer with examples.
3. It has been observed that software designers sometimes ignore, or make limited use of in-house guidelines. Discuss the reasons why this might occur.

Approach to answers

1. Here you would need to distinguish between different stakeholder groups, i.e. end-users, designers, organisations. The benefits to each group sometimes overlap, but by categorising the beneficiaries you will provide yourself with a framework which makes the points easier to remember. It might help to imagine yourself as a member of each of these groups.

2. Design principles tend to be high level (widely applicable and general); derive from theory and practice; underpin guidelines and standards – here you need to give some examples and explain how they are derived. Usability guidelines offer support to the designer to achieve adherence to particular design principles. They vary in terms of their

generality, but in the main they tend to the generic and are advisory as opposed to authoritative in nature – again, give some examples, not just of general, individual guidelines, but published guidelines such as Maguire (1999). There are many sets of standards, with different status (explain the different types) associated with IT in general and interface design and usability in particular (give some specific examples, such as ISO 13407). Usability related standards can be categorised according to their main purpose (explain these uses citing, for example, Newman and Lamming (1995).

3. Problems – tend to be either too general or too implementation-specific; difficulties for designers in interpretation of guidelines. Need meta-guidelines about how to make trade-off decisions regarding use of guidelines? May be inaccessible, poorly presented. May be contradictory or ambiguous. Designers may perceive that guidelines constrain creativity and innovation. And so on ... Here you would need to present evidence from the literature to support your answer, rather than just anecdotal evidence or personal opinion.

Section 5

Further reading and research

Further reading

Books and papers

Dix, A. *et al*. (1998) – Section 4.3 'Principles to support usability' and Section 5.3 'Using design rules'.

Löwgren, J. and Laurén, U. (1993).

Newman, W. M. and Lamming, M. G. (1995) – Chapter 15 'Designing to guidelines'.

Reed, P. *et al*. (1999).

Websites

European Usability Support Centre at HUSAT (Human Sciences and Advanced Technology) Loughborough University. *http://www.lboro.ac.uk/research/husat/eusc/r_usability_sites.html* (last accessed 24/11/02). A list of useful links to all kinds of information about usability, including guidelines and standards.

National Cancer Institute (USA). *http://usability.gov* Set up to improve the communication of cancer research. A perhaps surprising source of very comprehensive advice and links on usability. See especially the links to guidelines and checklists at *http://usability.gov/guides/index.html* (last accessed 24/11/02).

Interesting 'strength of evidence' scale for each guideline – see *http://usability.gov/guidelines/intro.html#3* (last accessed 24/11/02).

TRUMP. *http://www.usability.serco.com/trump/resources/standards.htm* (last accessed 24/11/02). Serco is a large, independent usability consultancy. This link contains an exhaustive list and descriptions of user centred design standards in connection with the TRUMP project. There is lots of other information plus links relevant to user interface design/usability.

W3C – World Wide Web Consortium. *http://www.w3c.org* (last accessed 24/11/02). Probably the most important standards setting body in connection with the WWW.

Further research

1. Research some of the resources relevant to the topic of this chapter and identify:

   (a) A set of **generic** design guidelines that could be **generally** applied to the design of any system.

   (b) A set of **specific** design guidelines that relate to a **particular** type of system.

   (c) Having read and understood them:

   (i)   decide upon the relative level of authority of the two sets of guidance;

   (ii) try to form some sort of judgement as to the validity and reliability of each set of guidance.

2. Familiarise yourself with the main processes that form ISO 13407 – you could do this by visiting some of the websites listed at the end of the chapter and following appropriate links. Now imagine that you have been commissioned to design a small system of your own choice (or perhaps one that you have been set as a class assignment) and sketch out how you would approach the task following the guidance laid out in the standard. If you are following this book in a linear fashion, there will be areas that may be unfamiliar to you at this stage, but complete what you can, and fill in the rest later as your knowledge grows.

Chapter 4
User requirements: elicitation and analysis

Chapter summary

The interface design process must start somewhere, but until a clear identification of the design problem has been established there is little point in actually designing or building anything. This chapter starts with a brief review of the idea of design models to which you were introduced in Chapter 2 and discusses the extent to which they might help (or hinder) the requirements elicitation process. It then moves on to consider a general process for the elicitation and analysis of data leading to the production of a problem statement identifying the requirements (the design problem) plus key usability and other design goals. The final section introduces you to the wealth of techniques available for data collection and explains some of the more commonly used methods in further detail.

Learning outcomes

Outcome 1: Understand the advantages and limitations that different systems development models bring to the requirements elicitation process.
You will need to understand the main features of generic design methodologies and be able to explain how the requirements elicitation process is enhanced or constrained by different models. Question 1 at the end of the chapter tests your ability to do this.

Outcome 2: Understand a general model of the requirements elicitation process and how this leads to the production of a problem definition.
Although there are many different methodologies in use, you should have an understanding of the general process of requirements elicitation and how this leads to the production of a problem definition report. Question 2 at the end of the chapter gives you the opportunity to explore this.

Outcome 3: Be aware of the different techniques used for data collection and understand how to apply some of the more common ones.
Again, there are numerous data collection techniques that can be applied to requirements elicitation. You need to be familiar with some of the most commonly used techniques and understand how to apply them. Question 3 at the end of the chapter tests your knowledge and ideas about this.

How will you be assessed on this?

For project work you would be expected to demonstrate that you had considered more than one development model prior to commencing the work and you should explain why any particular model had been chosen over another. Some additional research should be evident to enable you to apply the model effectively. Similarly, you would need to research appropriate data collection techniques and apply them successfully. You would need to be able to demonstrate some insight into the design problem by analysing and interpreting the data collected in a rational manner. Tutors will be interested in detail of the processes as well as the actual outcome, so documentation of all the processes and explanation of the rationale underpinning decisions is important.

In an examination you may be expected to compare and contrast different design models, requirements elicitation methods and data collection techniques. You might be expected to analyse and interpret requirements data in the context of a given, specific case study.

Section 1

Where do we start?

In Chapter 3 you became aware of the wealth of support available for the interface designer and in Chapter 5 the focus will be on practical methods and techniques for carrying out the design part of the process. In this section we will first review and discuss briefly the idea of design **models** to which you were introduced in Chapter 2 and discuss the extent to which they might contribute to the requirements elicitation process.

As mentioned previously, many variants of the systems lifecycle follow a generic waterfall model as schematised below in Figure 4.1.

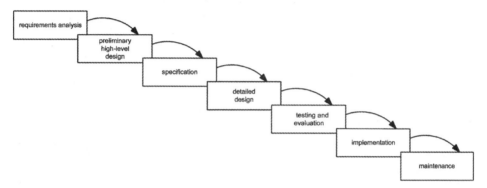

Figure 4.1 Waterfall model of systems lifecycle

In this chapter we are concerned with the requirements analysis stage. From a human-centred point of view, the waterfall model presents some problems. One obvious point is that the whole process hinges on a clear and accurate set of requirements – it is often very difficult to establish these requirements, which should extend beyond simple lists of 'features', for example: 'the system should provide a pull-down menu system' and so on. An interface designer will be concerned with establishing usability and other design goals and ensuring that the product meets these goals. So one good place to start is by thinking about the users' **goals**. Cooper (1999) offers an illuminating example of the difference between features and goals. He describes how a colleague, Scott McGregor, asks his students to guess what a particular product is by providing a list of its features, i.e.:

- internal combustion engine;
- four wheels with rubber tyres;
- transmission connecting the engine to the drive wheels;
- engine and transmission mounted on metal chassis;
- steering wheel.

At this point, most of us will have guessed that the product is a car. Scott then switches to mentioning a couple of user goals:

- cuts grass quickly and easily;
- comfortable to sit on.

In fact, what is being described is a ride-on lawn mower, although this is not at all obvious simply by looking at a list of its features. It can be seen, in a general design sense then, that features might best emanate from the user goals rather than the other way round, hence the importance of understanding the design problems (and producing a problem definition) before formalising them as requirements.

─────── CRUCIAL TIP ───────

The process of understanding the users, their goals and context of work can be thought of as identifying the design problems and producing a problem definition. In the context of design generally, the word 'problem' does not have its usual negative connotations.

Worth noting are some other difficulties associated with the waterfall method:

- the end user is often only involved at the requirements analysis stage (and may not be involved at all);
- the process can be inflexible, making iteration difficult;
- deliverables only 'appear' at the end of the implementation phase (by which time it is generally too expensive and difficult to make changes);
- usability issues are often ignored;
- the interface is often 'tacked on' as an afterthought.

Alternative design process models have been proposed, for example Hartson and Hix's (1989) star model, below in Figure 4.2.

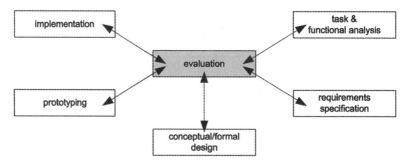

Figure 4.2 Star model of systems development (after Hartson and Hix, 1989)

The star model is essentially **iterative**, with **evaluation** at the core. Within reason, any of the main processes can be revisited as a result of information obtained during an evaluation exercise. By contrast, the waterfall method is generally implemented in a linear fashion, with limited iteration and, if done at all, evaluation is conducted at the end. So a key difference between the star and waterfall method is that the requirements specification can be informed and refined throughout the whole design process to ensure that a system meets particular usability and other design goals.

─────── CRUCIAL CONCEPT ───────

The **waterfall model** of the systems lifecycle depends on a clear set of user requirements – these are seldom revisited throughout the process; additionally it rarely incorporates any early evaluation and is essentially a linear set of activities. More appropriate and meaningful user requirements, and hence a more usable system, may emerge by deploying a **human centred and iterative development model** that incorporates usability evaluation throughout the process.

You will recall from Chapter 3 that there are emerging process standards focusing on a human centred approach and incorporating iteration and evaluation – ISO 13407: Human-centred design processes for interactive systems was mentioned. Figure 4.3 below is a schematic of the overall framework.

You will see that the overall process is again iterative, although it **can** be adapted to the waterfall approach by simply passing once through the cycle. The framework includes specific stages for specifying the context of use and also the user and organisational requirements; to an extent, many of the techniques described in the next section can be used for both purposes and also for the purposes of usability evaluation.

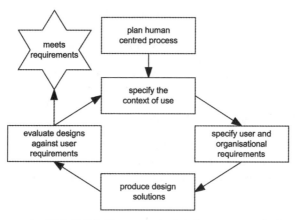

Figure 4.3. Framework of ISO 13407: Human-centred design processes for interactive systems

---
CRUCIAL TIP

It can be difficult to distinguish the boundaries between requirements capture, design processes and evaluation processes. For instance, if an initial prototype is built and evaluated, more may be learned about the user requirements – so would this have been a requirements specification, design or evaluation process? This blurring of distinctions is part of what makes interface design a dynamic process.

Notwithstanding an iterative approach, the interface designer has to make a start somewhere at producing a problem definition by eliciting and analysing information from the stakeholders. The next section will outline the type of information that could be included in a problem definition.

CRUCIAL CONCEPT

A **stakeholder** is anyone likely to be involved with and/or affected by the design, production and use of a system.

Quick test

1. What is the main problem associated with the waterfall method?
2. What are the key features of a development model that would enable a useful set of user requirements initially to be established and later reviewed/amended?

Section 2

The problem definition

In this section we will cover the information you need to obtain in order to produce a comprehensive problem definition report that clearly identifies the design problem and the goals of the system. Section 3 will introduce some of the many techniques available for eliciting this type of information, so you should think of this section as clarifying **what** you are aiming to achieve and the next section as **how** you could achieve this aim.

The least effective way of approaching an interface design is to jump straight in and start coding something. Remember that you are designing a system for other people to use – not yourself. It is essential to commence by conducting extensive research and establishing first of all what the design problem actually **is** and then identifying some key goals. The investigations will form the problem definition and should be written up as a report. You will find some useful guidance on what might be included, and how it could be formatted, produced by Maguire *et al.* (1997) at: *http://www.ejeisa.com/nectar/respect/5.3/contents.htm. (User-Centred Requirements Handbook.* Deliverable D5.1, Telematics Applications RESPECT project TE2010) (last accessed 24/11/02).

An illustration of what sections might then be included in the problem definition follows. The example used throughout is based on a real case study – the redesign (conducted by one of the authors) of a corporate intranet for one particular office of a government department with offices in many locations across the UK. The department is referred to here as Big Department, and the particular office is referred to as Local Office. Within Local Office there are various Divisions responsible for particular areas of work; each Division has a Divisional Rep who is responsible for commissioning, and in some cases actually developing, particular pages within the intranet.

CRUCIAL TIP

It is important to set the scene by outlining the structure of, say, an organisation as well as including a summary outlining what your report contains. You would need to provide a lot more information than was intimated above.

Summary of main stakeholders

In Chapter 1 the importance of understanding the characteristics of the users and the system's context of use was emphasised. One method of commencing this part of the initial investigation is to conduct a stakeholder analysis. At the simplest level, this could mean summarising the different individuals and groups of people likely to be involved with and/or affected by the system and their main task goals. Table 4.1 below shows an example of how this could be specified.

CRUCIAL TIP

There are many different ways of presenting the type of information shown in Tables 4.1–4.7. In your practical work you may be asked to present your research under different headings or in a different format, and some of the terminology may differ, but the basic principles would remain the same.

Table 4.1 Summary of main stakeholders

Primary users	Main task goals
Staff of Local Office	Easy access to up-to-date reference material Keep up to date with Local Office news
Divisional Reps (user/developers)	Keep up to date with Local Office news Access up-to-date reference material Be able to produce simple web pages for their Division 'Sell' the intranet to their colleagues

Other stakeholders	Main task goals
Intranet developers	Build web pages quickly Remain the primary expert intranet developers 'Sell' the intranet to content owners
Local Office Communications Team	Get the right information to the right people at the right time Avoid duplicating material and cut down on paper distribution Make information accessible to all staff 'Sell' the intranet to Local Office staff
System owner	Obtain VFM (value for money) Achieve a quality intranet that reflects well on Local Office Enable staff to serve the public more effectively and therefore achieve Local Office targets

Other staff in Big Department	Obtain information provided by Local Office subject experts Find out about Local Office personnel and responsibilities
(Future) staff in other Government Departments via GSI (Government Secure Intranet)	Obtain information provided by Local Office subject experts Find out about Local Office personnel and responsibilities

Having identified the key stakeholders, the next task should be to identify the characteristics of each user group and the potential implications in the context of system requirements. Table 4.2 below shows an example of how this could be presented for just one of the user groups.

Table 4.2 User group characteristics

System: *Local Office intranet* **User group:** *Staff of Local Office*	
Characteristics	**Potential system requirements**
Skills and knowledge	
Experience in:	
(a) using the current system All users of current intranet No formal training	Make system as intuitive and self-explanatory as possible
(b) using other systems with similar main functions Experience of obtaining information from databases, email and paper sources	Try to make the system conform with any accepted ad hoc standards for similar systems Use highly supportive interface with logical, clear structure
(c) using systems with the same interface style Most are familiar with the current intranet and many are fairly frequent internet users (% not known)	Ensure that interface adheres to de facto internet standards/guidelines
Education/qualifications Any level of ability	Design to attract people who may have few skills in use of the system
Linguistic ability All English speakers	Use English language but use non-technical language and terminology
Background knowledge/IT knowledge Variable, assume little	Use supportive dialogues to make user feel comfortable Use non-technical language and terminology Develop subjectively attractive interface
Physical attributes **Age range** 16 to 60 years	Make it simple for older (and other) users who are likely to be less IT literate
Physical abilities, limitations/disabilities Includes people with physical/visual impairments, some may wish to use text to audio translation software	Ensure text and controls are highly visible Ensure that all <ALT> tags are populated Provide text only version for important information

Mental attributes	
Intellectual abilities	
(a) differing information search/browsing preferences	Provide a variety of navigation aids such as A-Z index, site map, search engine
(b) specific mental impairments There are known to be several dyslexics who may wish to use text to audio translation software	Provide text only version for important information
Motivations	
(a) attitude to job and task Variable	Make information easy and quick to find
(b) interactions with others Generally quite sociable, interested in social activities and what other staff are doing	Include news of social activities and 'staff movements' Improve navigation of job vacancies page
(c) attitude to the system May be reluctant to use, many still like paper documents	Make intranet appear attractive and easy to use Ensure it is easy to keep content up to date Provide text only version for important information
(d) attitude to information technology Variable	Make intranet appear attractive and easy to use Provide text only version for important information
(e) employees attitude to the employing organisation Variable, but generally positive	Make Local Office intranet appear high quality in comparison with other Big Department sites so users can feel proud of it
Job characteristics	
Job function Variable – ranges from Messenger grade to Senior Manager	Ensure content is relevant and well structured
Hours of work/operation	Ensure that it is easy to see what information is new or changed
(a) hours of work Generally 'normal' office hours, but: many Intelligence Officers are only in the office 1 or 2 days per week and may work round the clock	Provide printable version for important information so that it is 'portable'
(b) hours using system Variable – probably no more than .5 hrs per day at present	Ensure content is relevant and well structured
(c) Discretion to use The aim is to put more information on the intranet and move away from paper-based documents	Make intranet attractive and easy to use Provide printable version for important information so that it is 'portable'
Other relevant features	
The Divisional Reps will also be doing some development work in the future. They, the Communications Team and the current intranet developers need to be able to make changes quickly and easily	Adhere to the general KISS (Keep It Simple, Stupid) principle with which all staff are familiar Keep coding of pages simple and well 'commented'
There are almost constant changes occurring in the Local Office's structure. Staff need to be able to identify who does what, and how the Local Office is organised	There should be clear organisational chart/s which are easy to maintain

We are now in a position to make some initial recommendations as to the functional requirements. Table 4.3 below illustrates this.

Table 4.3 Functional requirements

1. Improve the information architecture of the intranet in terms of grouping and labelling

2. Make information easily accessible to staff by improving and standardising the navigation elements

3. Create a more dynamic version of the *Weekly News* (the staff newsletter) on the front page that can:

   (a) be easily updated on a regular basis to create a different front page perhaps several times a day (to encourage staff to visit regularly)

   (b) be navigated and read easily from the screen

   (c) incorporate pictures of different members of staff and other images (to create interest)

4. The news items should be archived for future reference

5. The news items should be collated on a weekly basis and made available in printed format for staff to read away from the office

6. Include comprehensive A-Z index

7. Include TOC (table of contents) or other form of site map

8. Include 'browsable' organisational chart

9. Improve the navigation of the job vacancies page and make it more prominent

10. Improve the 'what's new' page and make it more prominent

Although Table 4.3 illustrated what is labelled as the **functional** requirements of the system, you will notice that the requirements have a major impact on the design of the **interface**, which is the focus of this illustration. We can now go on to be more specific about the interface requirements.

Other user interface requirements

Overall concept of the system
At this stage of a project it may not be possible to offer a very detailed concept of the proposed interface except to make some fairly general observations.

Table 4.4 Overall concept of system

1. As a preference has been expressed for a simple and clear interface, the use of a specific metaphor should be avoided. Another Local Office has used the metaphor of an office desk scattered with bits of paper and files; because it is very graphics heavy it is extremely slow to load and is very labour intensive to change. It has remained the same for more than 18 months, and observation and casual conversation with staff suggests that they are rather tired of it. Another point is that metaphor can be misleading and rather laboured in its effect.

2. The overall effect should be simple, clean and uncluttered.

3. To keep the front page looking fresh, it should be possible to implement frequent changes by keeping it relatively simple; it could be achieved by incorporating the *Weekly News* (it would be desirable to change this to *Daily News*) headlines in the front page. This approach would hopefully encourage staff to look in on a more regular basis.

4. It may not feasible, even though it may be desirable, to change the front page every day because of resource constraints. However, it may be possible to create a small area that could be quickly and easily filled with a brief 'news flash' when required.

Usability features

We are now in a position to specify some more specific usability features shown below in Table 4.5.

CRUCIAL TIP

Table 4.5 – do you notice a similarity here with the idea of principles and guidelines?

Table 4.5 Usability features

1. **Relevance**
   Information should be useful to staff and offered in the most appropriate medium.

2. **Content**
   It should be easy to see quickly what information is available.
   The content should be well written and free from spelling, grammatical or material errors.

3. **Subjective appeal**
   The pages should be visually attractive and enjoyable to use.
   There should be sufficient use of graphics to add to the overall appeal without making the pages awkward to update or slow to load.

4. **Navigation**
   It should be easy to get back to the front/home page from anywhere in the intranet.
   The information should be logically structured and labelled.
   It should be easy and efficient to find the information required (via use of different navigation aids such as TOC, A-Z index).

5. **Accessibility**
   The pages should download reasonably quickly regardless of technical platform.
   Text should be easy to read.
   With the graphics turned off, it should still be possible to grasp the information presented on the page.
   A text only alternative should be offered for important information.

6. **Consistency**
   The layouts within the pages should be consistent in terms of placement of navigational elements and wording of controls.

7. **Transparency**
   Before any action is performed by the user, it should be clear what will happen as a result.
   All hyperlinks should be visible and clearly distinguished, whether they are in text or graphic form.

Finally, we can identify some **specific** and **measurable** key usability (Table 4.6), and other design goals (Table 4.7) and think about how they can be **evaluated** to establish the extent to which they have been met. You will be covering evaluation in more detail in Chapters 6 and 7, but thinking at this stage about how the goals can be evaluated will help you with identifying clear aims.

Table 4.6. Key usability goals

1. Users must be able to use the interface with minimal help or instruction.
   This will be evaluated by:
   – preparing usability scenarios and conducting an observational evaluation with users

2. Users must be quickly able to see what information is available on the intranet.
   This will be evaluated by:
   – using a questionnaire completed by the users. The questionnaire will initially be reviewed by UID experts;
   – preparing usability scenarios and conducting an observational evaluation with users.

3. The information must be clearly structured and labelled – users must be able to find key items of information accurately by navigating easily around the site.
   This will be evaluated by:
   – conducting a co-operative evaluation with users on the paper-based prototype;
   – preparing usability scenarios and conducting an observational evaluation with users on the web-based prototype.

4. Users must be able to understand the content with the graphics switched off.
   This will be evaluated by:
   – using a questionnaire completed by the users. The questionnaire will initially be reviewed by UID experts;
   – preparing usability scenarios and conducting an observational evaluation with users on the web-based prototype.

5. It should be clear when each set of pages was last updated.
   This will be evaluated by:
   – using a questionnaire completed by the users. The questionnaire will initially be reviewed by UID experts.

6. The pages should load acceptably quickly regardless of technical platform.
   This will be evaluated by:
   – using a questionnaire completed by the users. The questionnaire will initially be reviewed by UID experts.

7. All hyperlinks should be clearly distinguishable.
   This will be evaluated by:
   – using a questionnaire completed by the users. The questionnaire will initially be reviewed by UID experts.

Table 4.7. Other key design goals

1. It should be clear who is responsible for the content of a particular set of pages.
   This will be evaluated by:
   – using a questionnaire completed by the users. The questionnaire will initially be reviewed by UID experts.

2. The pages should be visually attractive and enjoyable to use.
   This will be evaluated by:
   - *using a questionnaire completed by the users. The questionnaire will initially be reviewed by UID experts;*
   - *informal brief interviews following observational evaluation with users on the web-based prototype.*

3. The pages should appear fresh and up to date.
   This will be evaluated by:
   - *using a questionnaire completed by the users. The questionnaire will initially be reviewed by UID experts;*
   - *informal brief interviews following observational evaluation with users on the web-based prototype.*

4. The users should consider that the intranet contains information that is useful to them (or others) to enable them to carry out their work tasks efficiently.
   This will be evaluated by:
   - *using a questionnaire completed by the users. The questionnaire will initially be reviewed by UID experts.*

5. The overall design must be acceptable to the system owner and the communications manager.
   This will be evaluated by:
   - *demonstrating the paper-based prototype and the web-based prototype.*

A full problem definition would also include additional sections that are beyond the scope of this book, for example information relating to technological requirements and constraints.

CRUCIAL TIP

Always record any assumptions you have made. You may have to defend any design recommendations based on them, and you may have to change the design strategy in the light of further information. For similar reasons, during the design stage, all design trade-offs should be recorded.

Before you can jump into 'design mode' a lot of investigative work has to be carried out to establish a comprehensive problem statement. This research should cover the user group characteristics, functionality requirements, overall system concept, usability features, specific and measurable usability and other design goals. At this stage, you should also consider how the key goals are going to be evaluated.

Quick test

1. What are the main headings that should be included in a problem definition report?

2. What are the main characteristics of usability and other goals?

Section 3

Techniques for requirements elicitation

Having established **what** information you should be gathering and **why**, this section introduces you to some of the main techniques used for requirements elicitation.

CRUCIAL TIP

Many of the techniques introduced in this section can be used for design and evaluation as well as requirements elicitation. So while the generic term is 'data gathering techniques', in this chapter they are usually referred to as **requirements elicitation techniques**. You will be familiar with some of them in other contexts.

Before outlining the details of some of the more common techniques, it is useful to consider some general guidelines for their use. Preece *et al.* (2002) suggest:

- **Focus on identifying the stakeholders' needs** – what are their overall goals? How do they achieve them at the moment?
- **Involve all the stakeholder groups** – it is all too easy to omit the views of a particular group of people, especially end users, and it is important to understand how the constituent parts of an organisation fit together.
- **Involve more than one person from each stakeholder group** – you run the risk of just obtaining the views of one individual who may not be representative of the group as a whole.
- **Use a variety of data gathering techniques** – this will help you to achieve a degree of validity to your findings, plus different techniques yield different types of information.
- **Support the data gathering sessions with suitable props** – for example paper prototypes, storyboards, company documentation and so on.
- **Run pilot sessions** – important in connection with questionnaires to check for ambiguities, spelling mistakes etc. If you are working in a team it will save you potential embarrassment and a wasted session if, beforehand, each member of the team practises their role and how it interrelates with the roles of others.
- **Data recording is important** – if possible, all data should be recorded verbatim since people's interpretations of the raw data may vary. It is useful to be able to return to the source to review decisions, resolve disputes and so on. Video recording, for example is a very effective method since it provides a rich set of data, however it can interfere with the data gathering process itself and be very time-consuming to analyse.
- **Be realistic about what can be achieved with the resources available** – you will only have limited time, personnel, equipment, access to stakeholders and so on.

CRUCIAL TIP

It is unethical and even illegal, in some cases, to record people on any media without their full knowledge and consent.

There is an initially bewildering number of requirements elicitation techniques available. Again, you will find a useful summary produced by Maguire *et al.* (1997) at *http://www.ejeisa.com/nectar/respect/5.3/c.htm* (last accessed 24/11/02). This summary includes guidance for the following, in connection with what the technique is, when it could be used, application areas, benefits and limitations, method, process and practical guidelines:

- brainstorm;
- controlled testing;
- diary-keeping;
- focus groups;
- functionality matrix;
- group discussion;
- interviews;
- observation;
- paper prototyping;
- parallel design;

- rapid prototyping;
- scenario building;
- storyboarding;
- survey;
- task analysis;
- task allocation;
- video prototyping;
- walkthrough;
- Wizard of Oz prototyping.

Although there is not the space here to discuss in detail all the techniques available, it is worthwhile considering briefly those that are most commonly used.

Survey

Most surveys are carried out via the use of questionnaires that generally produce quantitative data.

CRUCIAL CONCEPT

You will find references in this chapter to 'quantitative' and 'qualitative' data; you will meet these concepts again in Chapter 6. **Quantitative** refers essentially to numerical data (generally characterised as being 'objective') and **qualitative** refers to more subjective data emphasising meaning over quantification.

It is particularly tricky to produce an effective questionnaire and since they are often completed in the absence of the researcher (who would therefore not be able to resolve ambiguities) it is especially important to pilot them before they are used for their real purpose. The format of a questionnaire would depend on its purpose (i.e. what is it the researcher wishes to find out?) but individual questions can generally be categorised as being either **open** or **closed.**

Open questions invite the respondent to respond in any way that they feel is appropriate, for example:

What don't you like about the current system?

One of the difficulties associated with open questions is that respondents sometimes reply with ambiguous or irrelevant statements, or cannot be bothered to write anything at all.

By contrast, closed questions restrict the respondents to selecting from a range of pre-determined answers. The researcher would clearly have to have some idea of the likely nature and range of responses in advance of compiling the questions (this is where piloting is often invaluable).

Closed questions take a variety of formats, the most common include:

Categorical: ranging from a simple 'yes/no', e.g.:

Do you have access to the internet at home? Yes/No

to slightly more complex such as:

Which types of software have you used?

Word processing	
Spreadsheet	
Drawing package	
None of the above	
Can't remember	

Rank order: sometimes it might be necessary to, for example, find out what particular features of a system are most valuable to the users. For this purpose, a rank order format would be most useful.

Place the following features of the Scribblelt word processing package in order of usefulness, where: 1 = most useful and 5 = least useful	
Search the internet	
Send document via email	
Dictionary	
Thesaurus	
Grammar checker	

Scalar: there are several different methods for formatting questions that involve scalar (or rating scale response) formats, for example a Likert scale as shown below, which measures the strength of agreement with a particular statement:

Key to responses:
1 – Agree strongly. 2 – Agree. 3 – Neither agree nor disagree. 4 – Disagree. 5 – Disagree strongly.

	1	2	3	4	5
1 I prefer using a paper company phone directory					
2 I prefer using an electronic company phone directory					
3 I am interested in hearing about social events					

Or a multi-point rating scale, for example:

Never   Frequently

	1	2	3	4	5
1 I look at the intranet					
2 The intranet is up to date					
3 I print pages from the intranet					

The above example demonstrates just one of the problems with wording a questionnaire – what might 'frequently' mean in this context – every day? Once a week? Skill and expertise are needed to produce effective questionnaires – there are numerous issues to be taken into account.

Focus groups

The focus group is a particular type of discussion-based group interview that is useful for obtaining qualitative data. Focus groups originate from sociological research carried out during wartime on the effectiveness of propaganda, and other types of sociological research into mass communication.

The general description of focus groups is that they comprise people with a particular set of characteristics focusing on and talking about an area of particular interest to the researcher. The sessions are moderated (often by the researcher) and tend to be relatively informal; they centre on open questions designed to generate dynamic discussion that may spawn new topics. Participants may also be required to complete a questionnaire. It is vital that the researcher is clear in advance as to exactly what type of information they wish to collect from a group. Some objectives might be to:

- explore possibilities;
- reveal areas of importance;
- prepare for subsequent research;
- understand a system user's domain and language;
- reveal users' subconscious motivations.

The focus group approach can also be used to supplement usability evaluation that has been conducted with individual users – to get some measure of the general effectiveness of a system, or to compare different designs. Focus groups do not replace, or constitute usability evaluation though, since it will generally be the moderator using the software and not the users themselves (Rosenfeld and Morville 1998).

Focus groups should ideally be perceived by the participants as unstructured and free-flowing. Nevertheless, the researcher needs to carefully plan and organise in order to maximise the quantity and quality of data obtained. The general method of implementing focus group research starts with identifying appropriate participants; this could emanate from previous stakeholder analysis. Since the researcher is often also the moderator, he or she should prepare a list of questions (open and/or closed) and topics beforehand. The moderator should, however, be prepared to be flexible during the process in the light of new and relevant topics that may arise. Having identified the required characteristics of the participants, decided on the main objectives of the meeting, and prepared a list of topics and issues, the interviewees should then be recruited. An ideal number of participants is between six and eight; this is based on evidence suggesting that group size is inversely related to the degree of participation (Millward, 1995). Because there is a strong likelihood that not all the people who have agreed to participate will actually turn up, it is wise to invite more people than are actually required. Suitable arrangements will have to be made in terms of accommodation, catering, and other facilities and resources. Nielsen (1993) outlines what he describes as a 'cheap way of approximating the focus group research' which is to use computer conferencing. He observes that some of the disadvantages of this method are that it is more difficult for the moderator to steer effectively, and that interviewees keen on using it are seldom novice computer users. Whatever method is used to conduct the focus group, the participants will need to be minimally briefed in advance, but care must be taken not to influence their thoughts on the topic to be discussed.

One of the moderator's tasks during the actual focus group session is to ensure that it is informal, relaxed, open and dynamic. To achieve this may require the moderator to posses certain personal characteristics – focus group research is relatively unusual in comparison with some other types of research; to conduct it to a high standard, the researcher needs to have a high level of interpersonal and communication skills. The moderator will have to manage the process so that each person feels able to participate, and to ensure that particular individuals are not allowed to dominate the group.

Interviews

Many of the aspects of planning and conducting focus group research apply also to interviewing; it should be reasonably obvious where the similarities occur. Many interview methods (including focus groups) can be categorised as being structured or unstructured. Structured interviews tend to pose a series of closed questions that, although limiting the responses of the interviewee, tend to make the interviewing process easier and the resulting data quicker (though not necessarily easier or more informative) to analyse.

The semi-structured (or 'flexible') interview, it could be argued, incorporates the best features of both structured and unstructured techniques. It enables the interviewer to start with some predetermined closed questions and gradually open up the interview to probe deeper into what the interviewee is saying. This method is also useful for following up a questionnaire exercise by, for example, interviewing a sample of the respondents to clarify certain issues and help ensure greater validity.

Observation

Observational methods, at the simplest level, involve a researcher watching people as they use a system and taking notes on what occurs. Observation may be either direct, where the researcher is present and can focus on areas of particular interest, or indirect, in which case events are recorded, perhaps on video, for future analysis. Indirect observation has some advantages in that it may be possible to inadvertently capture interesting events that could be missed if the researcher is focused elsewhere, additionally it can help minimise any effects, such as changes in behaviour mitigated by an outsider being present. On the other hand, ambiguities in interpreting what is being observed can often be resolved more effectively if the researcher is able to ask questions at the time (although some variants of the technique emphasise non-interaction between the observer and those being observed). Contextual enquiry (introduced in Chapter 2) could be regarded as an extension of observational methods, and is also participative in nature, since it involves cross-functional teams engaging with users in their work environment to fully understand the context of a system.

Some benefits associated with an observational approach, in connection with a corporate system, whether it be simple watching or a full on contextual enquiry, are that it enables a better understanding of:

- the users
  - their characteristics
  - how they interact with one another
  - their vocabulary
  - how they use other artefacts, such as paper, as well as IT systems
  - work practices;

- IT and other systems
  - how they interrelate
  - the benefits and constraints they confer;

- the organisation
  - aims
  - corporate culture
  - corporate vocabulary
  - structure
  - data flow
  - work processes;

- how people, systems and the organisation interrelate
  - internally
  - externally
  - formally
  - informally.

CRUCIAL TIP

There is a distinction between **practice** and **process** (as mentioned above). Process can be thought of as the way an organisation formalises the way things are to be done, in some cases to comply with certain quality standards. Practice is the way things are **actually** done by employees – in some cases subverting corporate practice – to facilitate a more pragmatic approach to getting the job done effectively and retaining some measure of control over what they know and do. An excellent case study, concerning photocopier engineers, which illustrates this idea, is presented by Brown and Duguid (2000) as part of some interesting research into how social knowledge networks and the nature of work practice should be understood before imposing IT systems.

Criticisms of these techniques include the amount of time required, especially to interpret the data, and its associated cost in terms of money. There are also opportunity costs to take into account, i.e. the time lost while employees explain what they are doing or interact in other ways with designers and researchers. Other critics are nervous about any field-based techniques, i.e. those that are not laboratory based and therefore not 'scientific'. There are numerous refutations of this particular objection including Lund (1997) who uses as a particular example, a user who may appear more 'productive' in a laboratory but who resumes 'normal pace' in the workplace.

CRUCIAL TIP

There exists a multiplicity of data gathering techniques that can be used for a variety of purposes. Skill and judgement are required to select and use effectively the most appropriate for a particular purpose.

A final note

After data has been recorded and analysed, an interpretation of the information can be undertaken. There are two main types of data analysis: qualitative and quantitative. Qualitative aspects tend to be relatively subjective and emphasise meaning over quantification. However, quantitative analysis can be used to generate numeric values to represent, for example, the frequency with which a particular word is used, or to classify certain groups of words; whilst this technique would appear to be relatively objective, it is still subject to interpretation, so the distinction between qualitative and quantitative is not necessarily transparent.

Without doubt, the most crucial output of the whole requirements elicitation procedure is the designer's expert interpretation of the information; it forms the basis for recommendations as to how to proceed, and informs the whole design processes. Whilst requirements research is intended to be as objective as possible, we have seen how this aim can be constrained by the inherently subjective character of the interpretation of both qualitative and quantitative information. That is why all raw data must be recorded as faithfully as possible, the methods documented fully and notes kept on the reasoning that underpins an interpretation. It should also be possible, to some extent, for another researcher to replicate the research for confirmation purposes. By adhering to this methodology, it should be possible for others to follow the thought processes of the designer and acquire some understanding of the logic behind interpretations and subsequent recommendations.

CRUCIAL TIP

There is a difference between analysing data and interpreting it. For instance, if you discover that 80% of employees 'never use' the company intranet, is this because there is no information of value to them on the intranet, or because they don't have access to a networked PC? In each case, a different interpretation could lead to a different design recommendation. The interpretation of bald statistics is more likely to be valid if the researcher uses several different information elicitation techniques, in this example a survey supplemented by interviews would assist with the interpretation of the data.

―――――― CRUCIAL CONCEPT ――――――

Data collection is followed up by **analysis and interpretation**. It is important to document all these processes thoroughly.

Quick test

1. Outline the most common formats of survey questions.
2. Would contextual enquiry be a suitable method if there were time and financial constraints?
3. What personal characteristics should an effective interviewer have?
4. What is the purpose of documenting the requirements gathering process?

Section 4

End of chapter assessment

Questions

1. Compare and contrast the waterfall systems lifecycle model with a generic human centred development model in terms of requirements elicitation.
2. Outline a general method for establishing user requirements leading to the production of a problem statement in connection with the design of an online banking system. Illustrate your answer with examples as appropriate.
3. Identify two data gathering techniques that would be suitable for use at the beginning of an interface design project and explain how they would be used.

Approach to answers

1. The waterfall model of the systems lifecycle depends on a clear set of user requirements at the outset that are seldom revisited throughout the process. You should add something here to explain the importance of identifying a clear set of requirements. Additionally, it rarely incorporates any early evaluation and is essentially a linear set of activities. Here you would need to explain why early evaluation is important and how the results can influence the requirements. By contrast, human centred models are characterised by their iterative nature and frequent evaluation starting early in the process which means that requirements can be identified and refined progressively. Give some examples of human centred models such as the star model, or the ISO 13407 framework etc.

2. You should cover: the stakeholder analysis, user group characteristics, functionality requirements, overall system concept, usability features, usability and other design goals. A fair level of detail would be required and obviously any examples given would have to relate **specifically** to the context (in this case, an online banking system).

3. Observation and individual interviews are useful at the beginning of many projects. Observation enables the designer to understand the users (explain), the systems in place (explain), the organisational context (explain) and their interrelationships (explain). Interviews can be used to obtain more detailed information and also to clarify the meaning of observations and add greater validity to interpretations. You should point out why it is useful to deploy more than one method.

Section 5

Further reading and research

Further reading

Books and papers

Beyer, H. and Holtzblatt, K. (1998) – Chapter 3 'Principles of contextual enquiry'.

Faulkner, X. (2000) – Chapter 4 'Making usable products'.

Hartson, H. R. and Hix, D. (1989).

Lund, A. M. (1997).

Newman, W. M. and Lamming, M. G. (1995) – Chapter 5 'User study methods'.

Preece, J. *et al.* (2002) – Section 6.4 'Lifecycle models: showing how the activities are related'.

Preece, J. *et al.* (2002) – Chapter 7 'Identifying needs and establishing requirements'.

Websites

User-Centred Requirements Handbook. http://www.ejeisa.com/nectar/respect/5.3/ contents.htm Deliverable D5.1, Telematics Applications RESPECT project (TE2010). Version 2.21, April 1997 (last accessed 24/11/02).

Usability Net *http://www.usabilitynet.org/methods* 'UsabilityNet is a project funded by the EU Framework V IST Programme as IST 1999-29067: a preparatory, accompanying and support measure'. Authoritative, high quality information, papers, links etc.

Further research

1. While you are completing the further reading and perhaps visiting the suggested websites, record all the different design models that you come across. Note down the main features of each model and draw your **own** schematic diagrams of each one. Indicate on your diagrams where you think any data gathering might take place.

2. Refer back to the further research exercise 2 in Chapter 3. You should have already made a start on sketching out how you would approach the design of your chosen system loosely following the framework set out in ISO 13407. One of the processes in the framework is described as 'Specify user and organisational requirements.' Commence this part of the overall process using Tables 4.1–4.7 in this chapter as a template for your own research.

3. Questionnaires are commonplace in daily life. Start a collection of them (it doesn't matter what the subject matter is) and assess how easy or difficult each one is to complete from the respondent's angle. Then consider the design from the standpoint of the researcher and think about what information they are trying to collect and whether you think that particular questionnaire is an effective tool. Make a note of how you think the design could be improved from both the researcher's and the respondent's point of view.

Chapter 5
Design techniques

Chapter summary

There are many different design techniques available to assist in the process of creating user interfaces. Design is a complex and skilled activity and few people are capable of designing user interfaces without the aid one or more design techniques.

The diversity of techniques reflects the variety of approaches to user interface design (see Chapter 2). Designers with an artistic background tend to use techniques such as storyboards and scripts; those from an engineering culture employ task and flow models. More pragmatic designers will use a combination of techniques depending on the precise nature of the user interface that they are designing. In this chapter you will understand and learn to apply several techniques that are commonly used to create user interface designs.

Learning outcomes

Outcome 1: Understand the purpose of and how to carry out task analysis.
Question 1 at the end of the chapter tests you on this.

Outcome 2: Become acquainted with certain dialogue specification techniques, such as state transition diagrams and statecharts.
Question 2 at the end of the chapter tests you on this.

Outcome 3: Become acquainted with scenario and storyboarding techniques.
Question 3 at the end of the chapter tests you on this.

How will you be assessed on this?

In an examination you may be asked to discuss how to carry out a task analysis or else to produce a simple task analysis on the basis of a scenario. You may be required to explain the benefits and limitations of using state transition diagrams (STDs) for specifying a dialogue sequence.

In your practical work you will be required to apply various techniques, such as STDs and storyboards, in the development of your own user interface designs. Assessment is likely to focus on the accuracy, thoroughness and creativity of your design work.

Section 1

The design process

In this section some inputs to design are discussed and a generic design process is outlined.

There are many possible ways of approaching the design of the user interface (see Chapter 2). Few designs are entirely unique and, in many cases, the designer is striving to produce a better, more usable product than currently exists. The starting point is to obtain information from a number of sources which will feed into the design process. These include:

- user requirements obtained from focus group sessions, interviews, stakeholder analysis etc. (see Chapter 4);
- observations of users working with similar products;
- design guidelines and standards (see Chapter 3).

A useful starting point is to model the range of possible tasks that a user is likely to want to undertake with the product. Direct observation of users working with similar products, supplemented with interviews, allows designers to undertake a task analysis exercise (see Section 2) which can provide an overall conceptual model of the user interface.

An appropriate next step is to apply the outcome of the task analysis to a description of the user interface in the form of a state transition diagram (STD) or a statechart (see Section 3). These map the necessary tasks a user will have to undertake onto particular states (or screens) and describe the user actions needed to move between states.

Once the overall design is established, the detailed screen layouts can be produced. The production of storyboards (see Section 4), based on information from user requirements, design guidelines and scenario exploration can be useful here.

It is dangerous to be too prescriptive about design. The general approach outlined above has guided the design work of the authors, but other processes are possible. Above all, designers need to be adaptable and creative in their approach, particularly if they work within the participative design tradition (see Chapter 2) where a high degree of user involvement will impact on design activities.

Quick test

What are the main steps involved in creating a user interface design?

Section 2

Task analysis

In this section task analysis is described. Task analysis consists of a body of techniques used for a range of purposes: with regard to user interface design, it is used to model and represent the procedural steps required for a user to complete a task with a computer and to achieve a goal. The validity of task analysis is discussed and the relationship between task analysis and design is outlined.

Task analysis can broadly be conceived of as a **family of techniques** for **representing information that will contribute to the design of human-machine systems** (Whitefield and Hill, 1994). It has been used in various forms for more than 40 years and employed in various domains, such as ergonomics, process control and human-computer interaction (see Stammers and Shepherd, 1995). It has also been widely used in the design and construction of training materials. Task analytical concepts are embedded in some software tools, such as UIMS and case tools.

One can undertake an analysis of what people do in their day-to-day work, for instance, for any number of purposes:

- to gain a general understanding of what they are doing;
- to gain some insight into the significance of their behaviour;
- for job redesign.

Or one can focus on how a task should ideally be carried out – perhaps one that doesn't yet exist – with the aim of designing the physical workplace, such as a manufacturing plant; or the interface to a computer application.

Task analysis has concentrated not only on physical activities, but also on cognitive 'tasks' (Shepherd, 1989). Various task models, such as command language grammar (CLG), task action grammar (TAG) and GOMS (see Chapter 6) aim at representing the knowledge needed to undertake effective interaction with a system, and are explicitly predictive in nature.

CRUCIAL CONCEPT

Broadly the purpose of **task analysis**, as applied within the context of user interface design, is:

- modelling the user requirements in terms of tasks to be carried out; and
- mapping the description of tasks onto specific design features.

The process of task analysis, in general terms, is as follows:

- data collection (often based on a set of observations of a source system);
- task description;
- task analysis;
- evaluation of the analysis;
- task design.

Ideally, we also need some evaluation subsequent to design in order further to establish the validity of the task analysis undertaken; and, inevitably, there will be one or more cycles of iteration involved (see Stammers and Shepherd, 1995).

Hierarchical task analysis (HTA)

This is probably one of the most widely used variants, possibly because it is so intuitive for many people. The basic idea is that purposeful activity is focused on the achievement of one or more goals (effectively, desired future states). To achieve a goal, one or more tasks need to be carried out, usually in some prescribed sequence. In a complex sequence, each task is aimed at achieving a sub-goal – a milestone on the way to achieving the super-ordinate goal.

A task, then, is a sequence of events, the successful completion of which results in the attainment of the relevant sub-goal. Events can be sub-tasks or discrete actions. So we have a hierarchical arrangement, with the super-ordinate goal at the top, and discrete actions at the bottom (Figure 5.1).

Particular species of HTA come with their own notation and terminology (e.g. in the GOMS approach, outlined in Chapter 6, tasks are equivalent to Methods and low-level actions to Operators (Card *et al.*, 1983)).

One further refinement is that to achieve a particular goal, there may be a choice to be made between two or more task sequences. Some task analysis approaches, notably that of Card *et al.*, acknowledge this in terms of selection rules – heuristics that can be applied to select between alternative methods.

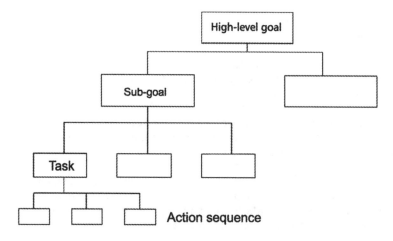

Figure 5.1 Indicative HTA decomposition

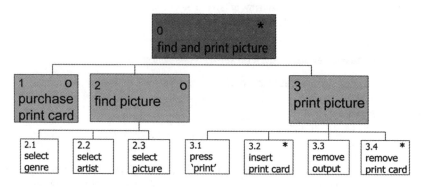

Figure 5.2 HTA representing fragment of a museum catalogue system for public use

Figure 5.2 shows part of a hierarchical task analysis of a museum catalogue system. The super-ordinate goal is to find and print a picture of an artefact from the catalogue. Tasks 1 and 2 (purchase print card and find picture) can be done in either order and this is denoted by the 'o' symbol in the task boxes. Note that a further symbol (the '*') is used in this example to denote repetition.

Levels of description

Potentially, we can describe activities at a very low level of granularity – hitting particular keys, defining mouse selections in terms of screen co-ordinates etc. There is an enormous amount of work to be done to achieve this, and in practical terms the disadvantages are likely to outweigh the benefits. There needs to be a judgement made of what the lowest level should be in the context of the use to which the task analysis is to be put. Shepherd (1989) discusses a heuristic to help decide at which level a task analysis should stop (p. 22). Broadly, the rule of thumb is that the bottom level of analysis should support specific design decisions.

Problems with task analysis

One major problem is the possibility of mis-match between the designer's model of the application and that of the user of the application (see Carey et al., 1989). There is a consistent and marked tendency for designers to conceptualise their design at the level of mechanisms (data handling and transformation; sequence of procedures) and object selection (video clips, text files, image files, for instance).

Users' models of the system or application vary in terms of levels. At the lowest level, this model is procedural – users know what they want to do and may have some clue about the mechanical procedures for achieving that goal (e.g. moving to a particular icon and clicking on it); but without having much idea of why a particular action sequence is successful or not. Higher or conceptual-level models probably imply that users form a fairly rich representation of what is happening 'behind the scenes' – a so-called 'mental model'. Development of an appropriate and sufficiently rich mental model is dependent on a number of factors, two of which are:

- previous experience with similar applications;
- the way the system presents itself to the user (adopting an appropriate and consistent metaphor, for example).

CRUCIAL CONCEPT

A **mental model** is an idiosyncratic cognitive representation that the user builds up regarding the nature of the system with which he or she is interacting. It is believed to be used predictively to guide user behaviour.

To the extent that the respective models of the designer and user coincide, design is likely to be successful. It is important, therefore, for the designer to put him or herself in to the user's shoes – to attempt to form a clear picture of the task from the user's perspective.

Other problems relate to the validity of the results of the task analysis process. This can be addressed in at least two ways: **content validity**, where the main question being asked is: 'Is the analysis correct?' (are there logical errors in the analysis?); and **construct validity**, where the emphasis is: 'Is the analysis appropriate?' (is it addressing the salient aspects of the task domain?).

CRUCIAL TIP

It is very important to validate the task analysis: all subsequent design activity depends on its accuracy. Both content and construct validity can be established by checking the analysis with representative users.

Task design

Once the analysis has been completed and evaluated, the next step is to produce a design. There is no prescriptive way of doing this, but Stammers and Shepherd (1995) make some useful suggestions, e.g.:

- the analysis should allow the identification of functionally related task elements, which can then be grouped together in some way (perhaps as either menu options or iconic representations on a particular screen);

- it should help uncover interrelationships between task elements, which might suggest a design allowing quick and easy access of certain screens at various points within the dialogue;

- it should support consistency in design (for instance making sure that similar tasks are carried out in similar ways);

- it should identify critical actions, which can then be treated in special ways in the design of the interface (e.g. message boxes if a user is proposing deleting a file);

- the frequency of occurrence of particular tasks and actions might be indicative of their relative importance and might demand priority in the design.

Quick test

1. What are the two types of validity associated with task analysis?

2. What are the main features of hierarchical task analysis (HTA)?

Section 3

Dialogue specification techniques

There exists a range of techniques which support designers in specifying, with some precision, the dialogue between user and system at the user interface. These techniques, usually derived from software engineering or knowledge engineering domains, possess particular notations, many of them graphical in nature. Certain of these techniques have been built into software tools, such as UIMS (see Chapter 2), in order to automate aspects of the design process.

Task analysis allows designers to understand the necessary tasks and actions that need to be supported in the design. At the bottom level of the task analysis, specific action strings can be identified. These can now be implemented as actual design ideas.

Clearly, at this point, design is a creative process. However, there is a range of techniques that can be employed to assist in the design process. For many people, applying these techniques is a stimulus to thought – creative ideas can quickly be generated, evaluated, discarded or enhanced. There is no particular prescription when to use these techniques – they need to be matched to the purpose of the design, and the choice of techniques is dependent on the preferences and experience of the designer.

STD (sometimes referred to at state transition networks) is a notation that can be used to model the flow of interaction within a dialogue between user and system (see Wasserman, 1985; Phillips, 1994; Clarke and Crum, 1994). The system, at any point in time, can be in one of a large number of possible states. In practice, a state is usually synonymous with a particular screen display, and can be described at various levels of detail. Transitions are those actions, usually made by users, which cause the system to change states. The whole dialogue can be built up as a network diagram, with states depicted as nodes (circles) and transitions as arrowed lines (arcs):

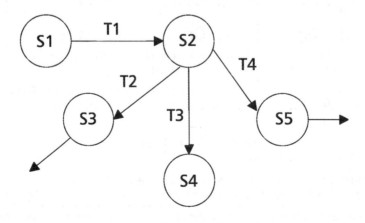

Figure 5.3 A simple STD

Descriptions of the states and transition are maintained in accompanying tables:

Table 5.1 Sample STD state and transition descriptions

State	Description	Transition	Description
1	Welcome screen	1	Select 'continue' button
2	High-level menu	2	Select option 1
3	Menu option 1	3	Select option 2
4	Menu option 2	4	Select option 3
5	Menu option 3		

STDs can be useful aids to design, but they have a number of limitations: the relationships between objects within states are not defined and complex representations lead to an explosion in numbers of states and transitions to be represented.

Harel (1988) proposed an extension and refinement of the STD techniques in terms of 'statecharts'. Horrocks (1999) presents a powerful description and advocacy of statecharts. Some prominent characteristics of statecharts are:

- They have a simple yet expressive diagrammatic notation.

- The states can be hierarchically arranged, which means that lower-level details can be specified later in the design; and that several states which allow access to a further state via the same transition can be clustered together diagrammatically, thus simplifying the network diagram.

- They can handle concurrency, a major feature of graphical user interfaces, where users can perform actions on several independent controls at the same time, resulting in multiple possible outcomes. An example cited by both Horrocks (1999) and Dix et al. (1998) is the provision, in modern word processor software, to change the appearance of text by toggling the bold, italic and underline buttons. Each function can exist in either of two states, on and off. Because these functions are independent of each other, there are eight (2^3) possible state combinations. Using STDs, each of the eight possible states would need explicitly to be represented; with statecharts, the information can be elegantly represented in one diagram.

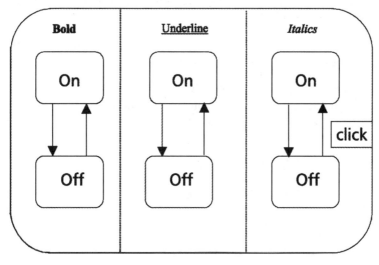

Figure 5.4 Statechart demonstrating concurrency (after Horrocks, 1999)

Other dialogue specification techniques are discussed by Clarke and Crum (1994), Phillips (1994) and Dix *et al*. (1998). They include:

- context free grammars, such as Backus-Naur form (BNF);
- event based techniques;
- Petri nets;
- flow charts;
- formal notations, such as communicating sequential processes (CSP).

Several of these techniques are very powerful in the sense that a very precise dialogue description can be produced and used to generate program code. However, they can require significant expertise to understand and use effectively. A related consideration is that complex specifications produced with these techniques are not necessarily ideal mechanisms to support communication of design concepts to end-users.

Quick test

What are the main limitations of STDs?

Section 4

Creative design techniques

This section looks at a range of loosely related design methods that are widely used within the participative design tradition (see Chapter 2; and Mountford, 1990).

Scenarios

These are little fictional stories – narratives – that allow designers to explore design ideas in particular situations (Carroll *et al*., 1994). Scenario development seems to be a natural and universal way that humans understand, plan and resolve complexity: most of us can imagine and 'run through' future imagined situations in our minds. Typically designers will outline a scenario to potential users and ask them to envisage what actions they would need to undertake (and in what sequence) in order to complete a task. The verbal responses of the users can then be analysed and a user interface interaction sequence can be modelled.

For example, if a designer is involved in creating a user interface to an ATM (automated teller machine) he or she will create some scenarios related to how people use ATMs. Users are asked to elaborate on the scenario ('In order to obtain some cash, I need to produce my card, enter the PIN number, select the cash option …' etc.). Analysis of the scenario helps designers focus on the optimum flow of interaction or dialogue sequence. Question 1 at the end of the chapter gives you the opportunity to explore an ATM example in more detail.

Scripts

A script is similar to a scenario in that it is a conceptualisation of necessary activities to achieve a goal. It is 'tighter' than a scenario, in that it describes actions without narrative padding and emphasises the correct order or sequence of activities. Schank and Abelson (1977) discuss scripts in some detail and suggest that we have mental access to a range of scripts appropriate for different situations. By exploring users' scripts, designers can produce interface designs, which map onto users' models of the world.

Metaphor construction

Often, it can be useful for a designer to establish an overall conceptualisation of what the finished design will be like. This can be translated into an explicit metaphor, which hopefully will map onto the user's mental model of the system and the interactional process. The predominant metaphor of recent years has been the desktop – the system presents itself as an analogue of the physical desktop, supporting activities relating to deskwork and depicting objects found on the desktop (files, drawing implements etc.).

CRUCIAL CONCEPT

A **metaphor** is a device for presenting new concepts via a representation of a familiar, real-world framework.

Many other types of metaphor have been used in user interfaces to different types of products: location-oriented metaphors for multi-user co-operative working applications, book metaphors for training applications and so on.

How do we decide upon a particular metaphor? We could think of a metaphor first and then attempt to make specific design features fit within the metaphor. However, Waterworth *et al.* (1993) suggest that, particularly for multimedia and hypermedia applications, the optimum approach is from the bottom up: defining low-level features and combining them into an overall model via intermediate 'micro-models'.

CRUCIAL TIP

Metaphors can be very useful for the construction of appropriate mental models. However, metaphors which are inappropriate or internally inconsistent can cause users significant problems (see *www.iarchitect.com* for examples of poor metaphor implementation).

This view is echoed by Preece *et al.* (1994), who discuss the use of various sketching approaches which could be useful. By generating large numbers of pencil and paper sketches (effectively visual brainstorming), organising principles tend to emerge, which can suggest new metaphors. The ideas can be refined and further organised; and when sufficiently robust, turned into software prototypes to act as the basis of discussion and exploration with other members of the design team or with users.

Snapshots and storyboards

These are visual approaches, which can be used to describe and make concrete particular scenarios. Snapshots are images which present a single event; storyboards are sequences of snapshots, illustrating a series of events. Series of screen images can quickly be constructed, either by hand drawing or by using an appropriate prototyping tool in order to demonstrate the appearance and sequence of screen displays. Through demonstrating storyboards to users, they can be iteratively refined.

Storyboards can be useful in confirming designs with users, but designers often need more specific guidance to produce user interfaces than simply sketches of screens. In order to provide a higher level of specification, storyboards can be supplemented with detailed descriptions of screen layouts, perhaps along the lines of the following table:

Table 5.2 Sample screen layout specification table

Object	animated icon	list box
Duration	3 seconds	permanent until transition
Location	top right of screen	middle of screen
Size	1.5 cm square	4 cm x 6 cm
Content	rotating sphere	list of options

Quick test

1. What is a metaphor in the context of user interface design?

2. What are the benefits and limitations of storyboards?

Section 5

End of chapter assessment

Questions

1. Outline the general process involved in carrying out a hierarchical task analysis.

2. What are the limitations of state transition diagrams and how do statecharts represent an improvement?

3. Explain the purpose of using scenarios in design.

Approach to answers

1. Decide on the highest-level goal; establish sub-goals and tasks; decompose each task into discrete action sequences. Need to establish the validity of the analysis when complete.

2. STDs of any degree of complexity are difficult to construct, understand and maintain. They cannot easily cope with graphical user interfaces, particularly features such as concurrency. Statecharts represent information much more concisely and elegantly and can handle concurrent events.

3. Scenarios allow users to run through in their minds the likely sequence of actions. Users' responses can be analysed by designers and interaction models created, perhaps using storyboards.

Section 6

Further reading and research

Further reading

Books and papers

Carroll, J. M. *et al.* (1994).

Clarke, D. T. and Crum, G. P. (1994).

Dix, A. *et al.* (1998) Chapter 7 'Task analysis' and Chapter 8 'Dialog notations and design'.

Horrocks, I. (1999) Chapter 1 'Introduction' and Chapter 6 'The statechart notation'.

Mullet, K. and Sano, D. (1995) Chapter 2 'Elegance and simplicity'.

Newman, W. M. and Lamming, M. G. (1995) Chapter 11 'User interface notations'.

Preece, J. *et al.* (1994) Chapter 22 'Envisioning design'.

Preece, J. *et al.* (2002) Chapter 8 'Design, prototyping and construction'.

Websites

Yale Web Style Guide (2nd edition). *http://www.webstyleguide.com* Comprehensive and authoritative site design guide from the Yale University Centre for Advanced Instructional Media. Also available in book form (Lynch and Horton, 2002).

Information and Design. *http://www.infodesign.com.au* Information and Design is an Australian usability consultancy. The site contains lots of useful information about interface design plus free downloads to aid the design process such as a paper prototyping kit.

Formal Methods. *http://archive.comlab.ox.ac.uk/formal-methods.html* '... contains some pointers to information on formal methods, useful for mathematically describing and reasoning about computer-based systems ...'. Compiled by Professor Jonathan Bowen, South Bank University.

Further research

1. In Chapter 8 of Preece *et al.* (2002) you will have seen various examples of storyboards. You should now attempt to create a storyboard of your own based on the following scenario:

   A person finds that she has no cash in her purse and decides that she needs to visit an ATM. After finding a machine, she inserts her bank card, types in her pin number and selects from the menu. She receives her cash and a receipt, and then the bank card is returned.

   When the storyboard has been produced, think about how this could be the basis for a more detailed design for the user interface of an ATM. Reflect on the advantages and limitations of the technique.

2. Figure 5.2 shows a fragment of a museum artefacts catalogue system represented as an HTA. In conjunction with observation of people using the system, certain problems were revealed:

   - people do not always purchase a print card before they use the system, hence they have to interrupt their search to go and buy a card;

   - the card is rejected if inserted the wrong way round;

   - to print a subsequent picture, the card has to be removed and re-inserted.

   Analyse the HTA to determine what changes could be made to the system to eliminate/minimise the errors and then re-draw the HTA to reflect a more effective design.

Chapter 6
Usability evaluation: formative techniques

Chapter summary

Usability evaluation is a vital component of user interface design. However careful the process of design, one can never be certain that what is produced will assist the user in interacting with the overall application. There are many techniques available to evaluate the usability of designs and thought needs to be given to selecting the techniques appropriate for particular design circumstances.

An important consideration is that evaluation needs to be planned and integrated with the actual design.

Learning outcomes

Outcome 1: Understand the difference between formative and summative evaluation.
Question 1 at the end of the chapter tests you on this.

Outcome 2: Understand how to select and carry out particular evaluation techniques.
Question 2 at the end of the chapter tests you on this.

Outcome 3: Understand the purpose of and how to construct an evaluation plan.
Question 3 at the end of the chapter tests you on this.

How will you be assessed on this?

In an examination you may be asked to explain the difference between formative and summative evaluation techniques, using examples, or be asked to construct a detailed evaluation plan on the basis of a scenario.

In your practical work, you will be expected to produce an evaluation plan to help you evaluate your design. This will include proposing appropriate evaluation techniques, establishing and justifying sensible usability goals, selecting and briefing subjects representative of particular user groups, identifying resources and timescales, tabulating, analysing and interpreting the evaluation data and proposing consequent revisions to the user interface design.

Section 1

Approaches to usability evaluation

In this section the need to undertake usability evaluation is emphasised and the distinction between formative and summative usability evaluation is made.

Both during and after the design process it is very important to make sure that the user interface design that is produced is highly usable. Users need to be able to access the underlying functionality of an application. The user interface can be regarded as the window onto the application and that window should be as transparent as possible. It is important that users do not expend significant amounts of energy grappling with the consequences of inadequate design, such as ambiguous instructions, inconsistent layouts and confusing navigation, when their primary goal is to use the application to carry out some task.

Unfortunately, there are many examples of poor user interface design. Some applications are clearly released to the market with little or no evaluation done on them. A collection of examples of poor user interfaces is maintained at the following site: *http://www.iarchi-tect.com/mshame.htm*

It is well worth visiting this site to see the kinds of problems that users have to deal with owing to poor design and inadequate or non-existent evaluation.

Regardless of the design process that has been used to create a user interface design, it is very important to carry out a usability evaluation of what has been produced. We need to ensure that designs:

- match users' needs and preferences;
- enable users to work productively;
- minimise the cognitive load on users.

CRUCIAL CONCEPT

Cognitive load refers to the amount of mental effort expended by users whilst carrying out a task.

Formative and summative usability evaluation

There is a distinction between **formative** and **summative** approaches to usability evaluation. Formative evaluation is carried out at early and intermediate stages of the development process on early paper-based prototypes or on partially completed software prototypes (see Chapter 2 for a discussion of prototyping). It provides informal, often qualitative, indications of usability which can be very useful in determining whether the design needs radical revision or simply minor amendments. Formative approaches tend to employ low-cost techniques which can be easily applied without the need for significant expertise or training within the design team. Another characteristic of formative techniques is that the results of the evaluation can be relatively quickly analysed, and the results fed back into the design activity.

CRUCIAL CONCEPT

Qualitative measures are concerned with the quality of a user's experience with a product. Evaluators can look for emerging patterns or trends that might be indicative of good or bad design.

Summative evaluation is carried out at the final stage of the development process when the design is complete. It provides objective (often quantitative) measures of usability, often for marketing purposes: either to demonstrate that the design is better than those of competitors or to demonstrate that the design has met a particular usability standard (see Chapter 3). Summative approaches tend to use rather more formal and 'scientific' techniques than formative approaches. This means, though, that greater expertise is needed to apply them, the analysis of the evaluation data is relatively complex and consequently they incur higher costs than formative techniques.

CRUCIAL CONCEPT

Quantitative measures are those that produce numerical values, such as percentages or averages.

The ideal approach involves the application of both formative and summative techniques: regular informal testing throughout the process which feeds back quickly into the design, followed by a more formal summative evaluation once the design is complete. Sometimes the tight timescale of a project and the way that the development team is organised (see Chapter 2) means that formative evaluation is abandoned: the danger then is that major usability problems only come to light at a late stage when there is little opportunity to rectify them.

Quick test

What are the main distinctions between formative and summative approaches to usability evaluation?

Section 2

Evaluation tools and techniques

In this section several useful formative usability evaluation techniques are described.

There is a large number of evaluation techniques available to the design team. Selecting the most appropriate is not straightforward and depends on a number of factors, such as:

- the stage in the design process it is planned to use the technique;
- the availability of usability experts;
- the availability of representative users.

Various classification schemes of evaluation techniques exist (see, for example Karat, 1988, and Whitefield et al.,1991). An overview of these schemes is presented in Christie et al. (1995) together with a discussion of how evaluation techniques are developing with the technical advancement of IT systems.

Some of the more widely used formative techniques are described below, while some summative techniques are described in the next chapter.

Predictive modelling

These techniques can be applied at very early stages of the design process, involving initial paper-based mock-ups of the user interface. The GOMS family of models (see Chapter 2) include a number of specifically predictive models that allow designers to predict aspects of users' interaction with alternative designs.

GOMS stands for:

- **g**oals;
- **o**perators;
- **m**ethods;
- **s**election rules.

As a user works with a computer application, it is assumed that he or she is attempting to accomplish a series of goals. In order to reach a goal, the user will apply one of a number of possible methods: sequences of discrete actions that, if carried out in the correct sequence, will allow the goal to be attained. The discrete actions are combinations of a small number of operators (such as key presses and pointing with a mouse). In some instances, goals may be attainable via more than one method. Users are assumed to choose between available methods by applying selection rules.

CRUCIAL CONCEPT

Selection rules are heuristics or rules of thumb, which allow the user to adopt the most efficient or appropriate method for achieving a goal.

A particular model within the GOMS family is the keystroke level model (KLM). This model predicts the user's speed of operation in accomplishing a task using a defined method. Each method is decomposed into a series of component operators. Operators have standardised times or a range of times associated with them, derived from empirical studies.

CRUCIAL CONCEPT

Empirical studies are those based on observation or experiment.

In the original formulation of the model (Card *et al.*, 1983) there were six defined operators:

Operator	Description	Times
K	Key or button press	Range (0.08 seconds for highly skilled typist to 1.2 seconds for totally unskilled typist)
P	Moving a mouse pointer to a target object	0.8 to 1.5 seconds
H	Moving the hands to the 'home' position on the keyboard	0.4 seconds
D	Drawing a straight line with a mouse	Variable
M	Mental preparation for an operation	1.35 seconds
R	The system response time	Variable

The time to accomplish a method is calculated by a two-step operation:

1. decompose the task into the sequence of component operators;
2. allocate appropriate times for each operator and calculate the total.

The times for alternative designs can then be compared. The assumption is that the design that takes the least time to accomplish a goal is preferred.

A simple example (after Newman and Lamming, 1995) illustrates the approach. Two alternative methods of emboldening a piece of text are:

- select the bold option from a menu;
- use a keyboard short-cut.

Assuming the text to be emboldened has already been highlighted, average times for the P operator and a reasonably skilled typist, the first method involves:

Action	Operator	Time
Point to format menu with mouse	P	1.1
Press, hold down mouse button	K	0.2
Point to font option	P	1.1
Release mouse button	K	0.2
Move to bold option	P	1.1
Click on bold option	K	0.2
Move to OK button	P	1.1
Click on OK button	K	0.2
Total		5.2 secs

The second method involves (assuming that the CTRL-b operation is performed by a skilled operator with the left hand):

Action	Operator	Time
Press control	K	0.2
Press 'b'	K	0.2
Release control	K	0.2
Total		0.6 secs

Hence a comparison of the times for the two methods indicates that the provision of keyboard shortcuts is a sound design decision. This example clearly assumes expert knowledge on the part of the user, i.e. that he or she knows the keyboard short-cut codes and the organisation of menu options.

The above example does not include M operators. Card et al. (1983) provide a set of rules regarding when M operators should be incorporated into the analysis. It requires experience on the part of the designer and evaluator to apply these rules consistently.

KLM analysis can be useful, then, in early stages of the design to help choose between design alternatives.

User walk-through

This is a technique that is used so that designers can see the operation of a product from the user's point of view. In brief, a user is given a specific task or series of tasks to perform using the product, and goes through it step by step, while an 'experimenter' records his or her behaviour.

Typically, a walk-through is carried out at an early stage in the development of a product, using a prototype, for example. The idea is that any bugs or ambiguities in the product are made quickly apparent by a user trying to perform the task. Similarly, any built-in misconceptions on the part of the designer – e.g. assumptions of knowledge that typical users do not possess – can be exposed at an early stage, and refinements in design can take place.

Also, walk-throughs are conducted on the completed, marketed products of competitors – to identify weaknesses which can be avoided when building one's own product. So walk-throughs are useful as a screening technique at early stages of the product design cycle.

It should be pointed out that there exist slightly different conceptualisations of walk-throughs. Booth (1989) comments on structured walk-throughs, suggesting that the designers, rather than users, walk through an envisaged series of routes through tasks. The user walk-through is closer to Booth's notion of simulating users.

Subjects

Some attention has to be paid to how you choose appropriate subjects. They should be representative of the target population(s) your product is aimed at. Normally, walk-throughs are conducted on a small number of subjects – say up to five people in each category of target users (secretaries, clerical workers, managers etc.).

To get some measure of the representativeness of subjects, they are usually asked to complete a questionnaire before undertaking the walk-through. This aims at obtaining relevant background information – age, job, experience of using various computer systems etc.

General procedure

A subject sits in front of a computer running the product and is supplied with a description of the task to be completed. Next to the subject sits an 'experimenter' or 'researcher', whose job it is to record the behaviour of the subject.

The subject then 'walks through' the product or package, attempting to complete the task. Subjects are briefed to act as naturally as possible, keeping up a running verbal commentary on their intentions, expectations and the consequences of their actions. Importantly, the subject does not maintain a dialogue with the researcher. The point of the technique is to study the unaided interaction of the subject with the product. The researcher will intervene only if the subject becomes irrevocably stuck or disoriented.

CRUCIAL TIP

Walk-through is a clumsy term. It implies that a user forms an image of the application and the task, and embarks on a cognitive journey through relevant areas of the user interface, attempting to complete the task.

What behaviours are important for the experimenter to record? These fall into two broad classes, physical actions and verbal utterances.

Physical actions:

- purposeful actions e.g. what key presses are made, selection of objects with a mouse;
- gestural behaviour e.g. apparently irrelevant behaviour, such as scratching the head, may be indicative of confusion. Care has to be taken, however, in interpreting the significance of such actions.

Verbal utterances:

- intentions – 'I intend to hit F1';
- expectations – 'I expect by hitting F1 to get the help menu';
- descriptions – of screen contents, for example;
- background information, opinion – 'I know another system that works like this';
- comments on effect of actions – 'I made a mistake there – oh, I'm lost!'.

While overt and verbal behaviour are easy enough to record accurately, their interpretation poses problems. In particular, the assumption that verbal utterances mirror underlying cognitive processes has generated a significant debate (e.g. Nisbett and Wilson, 1977). However, the analysis of verbal protocols in the context of user walk-throughs provides useful empirical data (see Scane, 1987).

Data analysis

So a whole mass of data can be collected, related to a subject's performance in using a product to complete a task. These data can give clues as to bugs or poor design, which would not otherwise have occurred to designers. Data analysis can be quantitative, for example counting and summarising the number of times different types of errors are made. Qualitative data are probably more illuminating: one can look for particular patterns of behaviour and match, for example, instances of uncertainty and hesitation to particular aspects of the design.

Heuristic evaluation

In this technique, originally proposed by Nielsen and Molich (1990), a team of evaluators (sometimes external to the design team, sometimes members of the team) are provided with a set of design heuristics which they apply to their examination of a user interface design. The design can be an early mock-up or storyboard, or a more developed software prototype. The evaluators independently review the design against the heuristics, concentrating on both the various screen layouts and the overall navigation of the user interface.

CRUCIAL TIP

Design heuristics are high-level guidelines, or principles of good design. Be consistent; provide feedback etc.

The comments of the evaluators can be recorded and subsequently transcribed, or else they complete a set of written checklists. The results of all the evaluators are aggregated and an overall list of usability problems is produced. The results then indicate areas of weakness in the design which can then be remedied.

Heuristic evaluation is an effective technique which can identify large numbers of usability problems. However, the technique requires the availability of a number of evaluators with some degree of knowledge and experience in the field of user interface design. In part, this is because interpretation of the heuristics is a matter of expert judgement: there tends to be some variation in determining what constitutes consistency, for instance.

Dialogue error analysis

This technique focuses on the possible errors that a user could make at each stage of the dialogue and identifying those features of the user interface which could be regarded as contributing to the error (see Christie et al., 1995, p. 334). The results of the analysis highlight facets of the interface that may need to be re-designed; or, if redesign is problematical, the analysis identifies possible mechanisms that can be built in to the design to help users recover from the error state.

The procedure is as follows:

(a) Perform a task analysis of the range of tasks the application supports (see Chapter 5 for an account of task analysis).

(b) Identify a method (sequence of action steps) to accomplish each task.

(c) For each action step of a method, identify all possible logical errors a user could make at that stage.

(d) For each error, identify those features of the interface which may be judged likely to precipitate the error.

(e) For each identified interface feature, propose a design change which would be less likely to cause that error.

(f) Assuming that not all changes can easily be implemented at this stage of the design, propose a mechanism for allowing the user easily to recover from the identified error state.

This technique is useful, since it highlights the gulf that often occurs in design, between the designer's conceptual model of the user's interaction with the design and the user's actual experience with it. Many of the faulty designs to be found in the *iarchitect* website referred to earlier in this chapter could have been trapped by carrying out a dialogue error analysis. The technique, though, requires a significant degree of expertise and time to carry out.

Other formative techniques (see Christie *et al.*, 1995) include:

- focus groups;
- questionnaires;
- interviews with users;
- physiological data analysis;
- usability metrics;
- critical event analysis;
- structured observational techniques.

Certain of these techniques, such as focus groups, are also used in the initial stages of the design process for eliciting user requirements (see Chapter 4).

Quick test

What is the aim of the dialogue error analysis technique?

Section 3

Developing an evaluation plan

In this section the need to construct an evaluation plan is discussed and the key elements of the plan described.

Usability evaluation, if it is to produce useful data that can improve the design, needs to be carefully planned, rather than carried out in an *ad hoc* fashion. Carrying out evaluation studies requires time, preparation and resources and, if a significant amount of formative evaluation is envisaged, the work needs to be synchronised with the explicit design activities. Some of the key issues in constructing the plan are:

- setting evaluation (usability) goals;
- selecting tools, techniques;
- establishing membership of the evaluation team.

Usability goals

Usability goals are precise statements of the intended usability of different aspects of the user interface design. Ideally, any design should allow users to complete tasks quickly and without making errors. In practice, of course, it is unrealistic to achieve a totally perfect design, often because design involves compromises: trading off one design principle against another. Also, a design that is optimal for one user, or group of users, may not be ideal for others.

The process of setting usability goals acknowledges that design perfection is, in practice, unattainable. The idea is to establish a range of benchmark values against which a design can be measured. If the design meets all or most of the benchmark thresholds when it is evaluated, then it can be assumed that it is adequate. Should a design fail to achieve a number of thresholds, or if it scores particularly badly on a key item, then the design will need to be revised.

> ───────────── CRUCIAL TIP ─────────────
>
> **Benchmarks** are quantitative criterion levels set in advance of the evaluation. If a usability test achieves the criterion level then that aspect of the design is considered satisfactory.

Usability goals need to be specific and measurable. They are often measured by exploring the behaviour of users with different aspects of the design. For example, if a designer is interested in the usability of a menu structure, a key issue is how quickly users can access items within the menu hierarchy. For a particular item, say two levels down the hierarchy, a reasonable time might be in the order of five seconds from the point that the users invokes the top level of the menu. There will be some variability in the performance of different users, however: some will take less than five seconds to target the item while others might take much longer.

The usability goal will then be stated along the lines:

'90% of users should access the information item in five seconds or less.'

If, in the evaluation, these thresholds (90% of users and five seconds) are achieved, the designer can have some confidence in that aspect of the design. If the thresholds are not met (say a majority of users is taking 15 seconds on average to locate the menu item), then it can be assumed that there is a design problem. This might relate to the overall menu structure, ambiguous terminology used for the item or some other feature in the user interface. Further exploration, perhaps involving discussions with users, will need to take place to identify the problem.

Often usability goals incorporate benchmark statements relating to users' errors. Errors can occur for a number of reasons: the amount of information presented at certain points in the dialogue may be confusing, terms used for particular functions are ambiguous and so on.

The usability goal stated above can be modified to acknowledge error occurrence:

'90% of users should access the information item in five seconds or less with an error rate of less than 10%.'

or errors can be explicitly measured without reference to time:

'At this point in the dialogue, error rates should be less than three per 100 keystrokes.'

Again, if subsequent user evaluation indicates that this threshold is not being achieved, it may be evidence of a significant design flaw.

How are usability goals established? Sometimes they are produced on the basis of the experience and best guess of the design team. Often they have some basis in the design guideline literature, usability standards or a style guide (see Chapter 3).

The virtue of establishing a set of usability goals at an early stage in the design process (see Chapter 4) is that an explicit quality assurance mechanism is established. Design becomes principled and focused rather than haphazard, and the quality can be checked both as the design proceeds and when it is complete. Usability audit instruments (see Chapter 7) often incorporate scores for a range of usability goals in order to provide an overall summative evaluation of a completed product.

Selection of tools and techniques

The various tools and techniques need to be related to the stages involved in product development. Predictive models are generally applied at early stages of the design using paper-based specifications or non-functional prototypes: their value is that alternative designs can be assessed before significant design and implementation effort has been committed. Walk-throughs and dialogue error analysis tend to be of more use once significant development work has been carried out.

Other issues involved in the selection of particular techniques are:

The use of multiple techniques (convergent validity)

It is useful to use more than a single technique at each stage. If, say, a walk-through and a heuristic evaluation produce similar outcomes, then one can assume the results possess a reasonable degree of validity. Of course, if the results from two or more techniques conducted in parallel significantly diverge, then a decision needs to be made as to which set of data to adopt.

> ──────── CRUCIAL CONCEPT ────────
>
> **Convergent validity** is the production of essentially similar results from the use of two or more different techniques.

Resources

Certain techniques are more resource intensive than others. Human resources include human subjects or end users, and expert evaluators. Physical resources may include a full-scale usability laboratory with appropriate hardware (computers, video cameras etc.) and software. The selection of techniques will be dependent, to a degree, on the resources available.

> ──────── CRUCIAL TIP ────────
>
> Many organisations concerned with software development maintain usability laboratories. These are specially equipped to carry out a range of usability tests on products in various stages of development.

Timescales

Timescales for usability evaluation need to fit in with the other activities in the overall product development process. In some cases this might mean that a 'quick and dirty' technique might have to be used.

Logistical considerations

Certain techniques may not be feasible to carry out in certain circumstances, e.g. difficulties in gaining access to appropriate numbers or categories of end user.

Ethical considerations

End users acting as subjects should not be misinformed or misled. Practices such as covert observation are nowadays regarded as unethical.

> ──────── CRUCIAL CONCEPT ────────
>
> **Covert observation** is studying the behaviour of users or subjects without their knowledge, e.g. from behind a one-way mirror. It is very important not to mislead subjects: evaluators should try to create an atmosphere of mutual trust and respect.

Membership of the evaluation team

The traditional model of the product development process involved quite separate roles, such as application developers, user interface designers and usability testers (see Chapter 2). The boundaries between these roles are becoming blurred in many product development environments because of the inherent inefficiencies of communication and decision making. As described in Chapter 2, certain participative design approaches regard end users as integral to the design and evaluation activities, often regarding them as co-designers. The more that everyone involved in the overall product development process has a stake in evaluation activities, the more seriously will usability evaluation be regarded and products will become more usable.

Quick test

What is the advantage of using multiple evaluation techniques?

Section 4

End of chapter assessment

Questions

1. Explain the key differences between formative and summative evaluation.

2. Explain how to carry out a heuristic evaluation.

3. A user interface design for a public information kiosk has been developed as a software prototype to the stage where a formative evaluation needs to be carried out. Provide a detailed evaluation plan to be carried out within the period of one week, so that the results can feed back into the next stage of the design process. Identify, in particular, evaluation techniques, subjects and timescales for each key activity.

Approach to answers

1. Formative evaluation takes place at early and intermediate stages within the design process. It employs a range of techniques that can be carried out quickly and without the need for significant expertise and produces results which can inform and feed back to the design. Summative techniques are more formal, require more time and expertise to conduct and produce results which are used to provide quantitative statements of the usability of a product.

2. Produce a set of heuristics derived from relevant guidelines; recruit a team of experienced evaluators and brief them; provide them with the design (either a storyboard or a software prototype); collect the comments of the evaluators and analyse the results; identify areas where the design needs to be improved.

3. The examiners will be looking for a sensible and realistic plan that will provide as much useful information as possible in the time available at a low cost. Key issues include:

   - selecting appropriate techniques (possibly a user walk-through and a heuristic evaluation);

   - identifying, recruiting and instructing expert evaluators (say two) and representative subjects (say five). For a public information kiosk, subjects will need to be as representative as possible of the target user group (a range of ages, verbal and interaction skills etc.);

   - the nature of the data analysis (which will include integrating results from the different evaluation techniques used);

   - sensible and manageable timescales.

Section 5

Further reading and research

Further reading

Books and papers

Christie, B., Scane, R. and Collyer, J. (1995) Chapter 12 'Evaluation of human-computer interaction at the user interface to advanced IT systems' in J. R. Wilson and E. N. Corlett (eds) *Evaluation of Human work: A Practical Ergonomics Methodology* (2nd edition). Taylor and Francis.

Faulkner, X. (2000) Chapter 6 'Usability evaluation'.

Newman, W. M. and Lamming, M. G. (1995) Chapter 9 'Prototyping and evaluation'.

Nielsen, J. (1994).

Preece, J. *et al.* (2002) – Chapter 10 'Introducing evaluation' and Chapter 11 'An evaluation framework'.

Websites

Usability Evaluation. *http://www.pages.drexel.edu/~zwz22/UsabilityHome.html* Summaries and links related to various evaluation techniques; includes a 'usability advisor' to help you choose a technique. Compiled by Zhijun (William) Zhang, Adjunct Professor at Drexel University.

http://utmk-ultra.cs.usm.my/pdf/apchi00.pdf 'A formative evaluation of scenario-based tools for learning object-oriented design.' A useful example of how to write up a formative evaluation process. Written by Hope Harley, Cheryl Seals and Mary Beth Rosson and published in the ACM's (Association for Computer Machinery) online student magazine *Crossroads*.

Further research

1. Refer to the further research that you carried out at the end of Chapter 2 in which you conducted a prototyping exercise. Design a simple formative evaluation plan to establish the extent of your PDA prototype's usability. Your plan should propose specific usability goals, particular techniques, an identification of who should participate in the process and a list of what other resources might be required.

2. Conduct the formative evaluation exercise in accordance with your plan. Reflect on how effective your plan was, in practical terms, for identifying usability problems.

Chapter 7
Usability evaluation: summative techniques

Chapter summary

Summative evaluation techniques are typically carried out towards the end of the design process in order to acquire information (often quantitative) regarding the usability of the finished application. This information may contribute to an in-house quality assurance programme, so that it can formally be demonstrated that products conform to local or national standards or contribute to marketing activities (to demonstrate that products are equivalent or better, in usability terms, than those of competitors).

There are other circumstances where summative techniques are employed. It may be the case that two or more alternative designs for some aspect of the user interface have been produced and the evidence from formative evaluation has proved to be ambiguous regarding which design is best. In this case a summative test may be used to produce a more objective, 'scientific' decision.

Learning outcomes

Outcome 1: Gain further understanding of the difference between formative and summative evaluation.
Question 1 at the end of the chapter tests you on this.

Outcome 2: Gain a basic understanding of experimental design and statistical analysis.
Question 2 at the end of the chapter tests you on this.

Outcome 3: Gain an awareness of summative techniques other than controlled product tests.
Question 3 at the end of the chapter tests you on this.

How will you be assessed on this?

In an examination you may be asked to describe how to carry out a usability audit or to produce a simple experimental design for a controlled product test on the basis of a scenario.

In your practical work you will be expected to produce an evaluation plan to establish the usability of your completed design. This will include selecting appropriate evaluation techniques (probably a simple experiment or product test), identifying and briefing representative subjects, describing the test procedure and the data analysis technique to be used.

Section 1

Controlled product tests

In this section controlled product tests (sometimes known as controlled user tests) are described.

It is often the case that a large number of factors are capable of influencing a user's behaviour with a product, and it may be important to isolate each factor and study its particular effect. The controlled product test allows us to do this.

The controlled product test draws heavily on classical experimental design, as practised in both the physical and the social sciences. In the social sciences, particularly psychology, controlled experimentation has, for many years, been the mainstream approach to empirical investigation.

There are particular advantages of experiments over other methods, e.g.:

- Because the experimenter is in control of events, he or she is generally prepared to make some observation. With non-experimental methods, there is the chance that events occur unexpectedly and are missed.
- Experiments are controlled situations. Hence experiments can, in principle, be precisely repeated to establish the reliability of results.

CRUCIAL CONCEPT

Reliability is a statistical concept which refers to the replicability of experimental results at different times and in different situations. If, for example, a test produces substantially the same results when repeated a week later, then the results can be said to be reliable.

On the other hand, the fact that the experimenter is controlling or manipulating events brings accusations that experiments are artificial; and that their results are therefore invalid. The results might not easily generalise to real life situations and may lack ecological validity.

CRUCIAL CONCEPT

Ecological validity refers to the truth of what happens in real life working situations with a product. In a brief product test, often carried out in a usability laboratory rather than in the user's own workplace, the user's interaction with a product may not accurately reflect what would happen in day-to-day life.

Experimental design

The starting point of many experiments is the initial observation of some phenomenon. Such observations are often incidental: something engages our attention, such as the observation that many people enjoy using multimedia rather than text-based systems; or they seem more productive or more efficient in using Version 2 of a product than Version 1. This casual observation might then lead us to formulating particular questions, e.g.:

- does this initial observation in fact reflect reality?
- if so, what particular factors in the multimedia system might be causing this phenomenon?
- What features of Version 2 are responsible for users being more efficient?

If we are sufficiently intrigued by the questions that we pose ourselves, we can then plan an experiment to find out the answers.

The following sub-sections consider some of the key features of experimental design.

Variables

As mentioned earlier, real life phenomena may arise through the interaction of many factors. Factors that vary to any extent, that is, can take two or more values, or be in two or more states, are called **variables**.

In a controlled experiment, the experimenter systematically controls and manipulates the values that certain variables can take; and then observes the effect of this manipulation on other variables.

There is a fundamental distinction to be made here, between **independent (IV)** and **dependent (DV)** variables. Variables over which the experimenter has control are known as independent variables. These can be varied by the experimenter to see the effect on other variables. The variables which are not controlled, but which the experimenter has an interest in observing, are called dependent variables.

There are hundreds of user interface features which can be treated as independent variables in product tests, for instance:

- menu organisation and structure;
- icon design;
- colour codes;
- command button size.

The state or values of these and many others can be manipulated in a product test in order to explore a particular hypothesis (see below).

Usually, in controlled product testing, the dependent variable is almost invariably some aspect of user behaviour. The most commonly used dependent variables are:

- time taken to perform some task;
- number of errors/ratio of errors to correct responses;
- numbers of different types of errors;
- attitude or opinion change;
- some measure of physiological response (increased heart rate, changes in EEG pattern, evoked potentials, palmar sweating etc.).

CRUCIAL TIP

The psychophysiological approach to evaluation holds that underlying cognitive events are reflected in changes in the body. By monitoring these physical factors, experimenters can judge the degree of arousal of subjects and make inferences about what they are experiencing at different points in the interaction with a product.

There are possible cases where the independent variable that is controlled by the experimenter is some aspect of user behaviour, and the dependent variable some aspect of system behaviour. Suppose we were looking at the effects of the number of users of a network on system response time. In this case, the independent variable would be the number of users – a variable which could be directly controlled and manipulated by the experimenter; and the dependent variable would be the time the system took to respond for each number of users.

By and large, though, in controlled product testing, we are measuring some aspect of the product with reference to how users behave in response to it.

Hypotheses

Often we might have some reasonable idea, based on our past experience or on a body of theory, of what factors are responsible for the phenomenon in which we are interested. If so, the next step is the formulation of one or more hypotheses.

CRUCIAL CONCEPT

A **hypothesis** is an explicit statement of what the experiment is setting out to test: in effect, a prediction.

For example:

Hypothesis 1:

'User satisfaction (DV) increases as the sound output of the product improves in quality (IV).'

or:

Hypothesis 2:

'User satisfaction changes as sound quality improves.'

Now, it is impossible to prove a hypothesis true. However many times one runs an experiment and gets the same result, this does not constitute a proof – there is always a possibility that a future run will give a contradictory result.

The way hypothesis testing is handled is to establish what is called a **null hypothesis**. In this example, the null hypothesis would take the form that there is no relationship whatsoever between user satisfaction and sound quality. The aim of the experiment is to test the null hypothesis. If the experimental results produce a result that allows us to reject the null hypothesis, then we are justified in accepting our experimental hypothesis.

Generally, we can reject the null hypothesis if there is a 0.05 (five chances in 100) or lesser probability that the results arose due to chance alone.

One- and two-tailed hypotheses

Going back to the hypotheses stated above, you will notice they are slightly differently worded. Both predict a change in user satisfaction; but only hypothesis 1 predicts the direction of change. Sometimes, in setting up an hypothesis, we can be reasonably sure that there is a relationship of some kind between independent and dependent variables, but not sure whether it is a direct or inverse relationship.

CRUCIAL TIP

A direct relationship means that as the value of an independent variable increases, the value of the dependent variable increases in proportion. An inverse relationship means that, as the value of one variable increases, the value of another decreases.

Hypothesis 1 is an example of a one-tailed test, while hypothesis 2 is a two-tailed test. An important consequence of choosing a one-tailed test is that the standard of evidence required to accept the hypothesis is somewhat higher than for the two-tailed test. Whatever hypothesis is adopted, is important to state it **before** the experiment begins and not to change it during the course of the test.

Operationalising variables

An important feature in experimental research is the need to precisely define what you are measuring in terms of dependent variables. If your hypothesis is that increasing sound quality leads to improved productivity, you have to operationalise productivity as a dependent variable(s). Efficiency or productivity is rarely a simple matter of the number of errors made or time taken for a task; but probably a fairly complex function of time, errors and possibly something else. Whatever algorithm is arrived at, it must be established beforehand on some basis other than your current results – possibly some pre-existing body of theory.

Subjects

The one crucial thing about selecting subjects is that your sample must be representative of the population to which you are attempting to generalise your results.

In terms of numbers of subjects, one is often restricted in controlled user tests. You may simply find it difficult or impossible to get a large number of subjects because they are simply not available. This is not too major a problem – but it does influence the type of statistical analysis that you carry out on your data.

Different experimental designs

We can make an initial distinction here between cross-sectional and longitudinal designs:

Cross-sectional designs

The behaviour of human beings is highly variable. One cannot make general rules about a phenomenon on the basis of observing one individual. Hence the standard approach is to involve a number of subjects in a one-off experiment, and to produce a range of descriptive statistics regarding their performance data: means, medians, standard distributions etc. This approach is known as a cross-sectional design, and the results are used to generalise to the wider population of which the subjects form part.

There are two main approaches (see Dix *et al.*, 1998):

- between-group designs, where each subject is randomly allocated to a group (in the simplest case, to the experimental group or the control group);
- within-group designs, where each subject will experience each condition in turn.

Both have advantages and problems associated with them: between-group designs require large numbers of subjects to minimise the effects of individual differences while within-group designs can suffer from learning effects: subjects will tend to perform better on later experimental trials since they have previously been exposed to the product.

Longitudinal design

Sometimes, for example if you are interested in studying processes of change – learning or adaptation – a longitudinal design is used. Here, although you may have a number of subjects, each undertakes the experiment, or a variant of it, on several occasions, perhaps over a period of months. The experimental comparison is made on the basis of different data sets from the same subject – not averaging data from several subjects – to understand how each subject's behaviour is changing over time.

More complex designs will look at variations **within** individuals and **between** subjects in the same experiment.

There is a large number of sophisticated experimental designs available. The simplest is a one-factor design, where you vary one independent variable and look at changes in a single dependent variable.

Control groups

It is often important to have a control group, as well as an experimental group of subjects. There may be a whole range of factors in the experimental situation which are potentially capable of influencing the results, but which are not themselves of interest.

So a control group would experience exactly the same procedure as the experimental group, except that they do not receive the experimental treatment. For example, drug trials routinely use control groups – those who receive a placebo instead of the experimental drug.

Randomisation

It is often important to randomise the order in which experimental material is presented. If this is not done, it is possible that something about the order can suggest or bias the response.

It is also sometimes important to randomly allocate subjects to different experimental and control groups.

Quick test

What is the purpose of using a control group?

Section 2

Statistical analysis

The quantitative data produced in a controlled product test needs to be analysed statistically in order that conclusions can be drawn. Descriptive statistics allow differences or associations between scores and variables to be summarised; the application of inferential statistical tests help evaluators judge the likelihood of whether the results are due to chance or reflect a genuine effect.

Descriptive statistics

The initial analysis of quantitative experimental data describes various characteristics of a data set. Say we have produced a hypermedia computer-assisted learning (CAL) tutorial application which has been used by 20 subjects. Let us assume that learners have some discretion in terms of navigating through the application; and that we have built in some logging software which can measure the amount of video accessed (in seconds). There are several descriptive measures we can derive from the data:

- the range;
- the average (mean);
- the mode;
- the median;
- the standard deviation.

Here is the data set:

Subject no.	Amount of video accessed (secs.)	Subject no.	Amount of video accessed (secs.)
1	34	11	27
2	45	12	28
3	21	13	19
4	24	14	31
5	42	15	38
6	34	16	32
7	28	17	41
8	29	18	49
9	57	19	25
10	28	20	56

95

To work out the **range** we take the lowest value (19) and the highest value (57) and subtract one from the other (57–19 = 38).

The **mean** is calculated by adding all the scores together and dividing by the number of subjects (20). The total of all the scores in this example is 688; so the mean is 688/20 = 34.4.

Sometimes we might need to establish the **mode** for a data set. The mode, in this example, is the score which the greatest number of people share. We can see that two people (Subjects 1 and 6) have scored 34; but that three people (Subjects 7, 10 and 12) have scored 28. The mode, then, is 28.

The **median** is another measure of central tendency. This is worked out by ranking the scores from the lowest to the highest, and reading off the score of the middle person in the sample. If there were 21 respondents, the median would be the score of the eleventh person; as there are, in fact, 20 people, the median is the average of the tenth and eleventh subjects' score. The lowest score in this sample is 19 (S.13); the next lowest is 21 (S.3); the tenth lowest (S.14) is 31 and the eleventh lowest (S.16) is 32. So the median is 31.5 ((32+31)/2).

CRUCIAL TIP

The median is a more appropriate measure of central tendency when the data is very skewed towards one end of the distribution. This is because a small number of extreme values can influence the value of the mean.

If we had a very large number of subjects and the scores were normally distributed, the values for the mean, mode and median would be very close together.

CRUCIAL CONCEPT

A **normally distributed data set** reflects the natural variability of many factors. Most scores will be close to the mean; a smaller number will be somewhat greater or less than the mean value.

Standard deviation is a measure of how widely spread the scores are around the mean. A small standard deviation means that nearly all the scores are close to the mean; a large standard deviation indicates that a number of the scores are a long way away from the mean.

Inferential statistics

The purpose of inferential statistical tests is to draw conclusions about data relating to a population by observing just a sub-set, or sample, of the population. They allow us to make inferences about whether difference in scores between samples are due to some genuine, underlying difference, or whether the results have arisen through chance.

There are two broad classes of inferential statistical tests: **parametric** and **non-parametric**. Parametric tests make certain assumptions about a data set, essentially that the data is normally distributed.

Non-parametric tests make fewer assumptions. In general, in controlled product testing, non-parametric tests are used, since it is difficult, with the types and numbers of subjects commonly used, to establish whether samples reflect a normal distribution, or whether scores from different samples have the same standard distributions. Whereas parametric tests tend to focus on differences between sample means, non-parametric tests focus on medians and **ranks** of scores, rather than their actual arithmetical values.

Inferential tests broadly look for one of two things:

- differences between sample scores (analysis of variance);
- association between variables (measures of correlation).

An excellent introduction to non-parametric statistics is provided by Siegel (1956).

Here we look at an example of a non-parametric test of correlation. Good examples of tests of differences between samples (t tests) are provided in both Newman and Lamming (1995) and Dix et al. (1998).

An important analysis that can be performed is to compare the effects of one variable on another, or to compare the interrelationship between variables. Say we are analysing some experimental data to do with the hypermedia CAL application referred to earlier. We wish to know whether the amount of video material accessed by the learner in a tutorial session has some relationship with performance on a subsequent test of learning. The specific hypothesis would be that the less video accessed, the more errors are made in the subsequent test. Here is a hypothetical data set:

Subject no.	Amount of video accessed (secs.)	No. of errors made
1	23	84
2	54	32
3	32	54
4	53	17
5	17	94
6	24	76
7	27	77
8	46	63
9	42	21
10	38	40

By looking at the data, it would seem that the hypothesis is likely to be correct: in general, the less video accessed results in the most errors. However, in order to be more certain, we can carry out a statistical test, to see whether the pattern is likely to have arisen by chance or reflects some underlying reality. The test to be used here is a test of **correlation**: as one variable increases in value, the other increases or decreases in proportion. The particular test used here is the **Spearman rank correlation coefficient**.

First we have to rank the two data sets. The lowest video score is given the lowest rank; the highest error score also gets the lowest rank:

Subject no.	Amount of video accessed (secs.)	No. of errors made	Rank of video scores	Rank of error scores
1	23	84	2	2
2	54	32	10	8
3	32	54	5	6
4	53	17	9	10
5	17	94	1	1
6	24	76	3	4
7	27	77	4	3
8	46	63	8	5
9	42	21	7	9
10	38	40	6	7

The next step is to subtract the video rank score from the error rank score, ignoring pluses or minuses. This gives:

Subject no.	Difference of scores
1	0
2	2
3	1
4	1
5	0
6	1
7	1
8	3
9	2
10	1

We now square all the scores and add up the squared values:

Subject no.	Difference of scores	Differences squared
1	0	0
2	2	4
3	1	1
4	1	1
5	0	0
6	1	1
7	1	1
8	3	9
9	2	4
10	1	1
	TOTAL	22

The formula for calculating the correlation coefficient (r_s) is:

$$r_s = 1 - (6 * 22/ (N^3 - N))$$

Where N is the number of cases (ten people in this example).

So:

$$r_s = 1 - (132/(1000 - 10)) = (1 - 0.133) = \mathbf{0.867}$$

By checking in a table of critical values, we can see that the obtained value for r_s is greater than the critical value for ten subjects (0.746 at the .01 level of significance). This means that there is less than one chance in a hundred that the result was obtained by chance, and we have confidence in saying that the amount of video accessed is inversely correlated with the number of errors – or in everyday terms, the more video shown, the better the learning.

There are many more inferential statistical tests that can be carried out on varied data sets; many of which can easily be performed using spreadsheet packages.

Quick test

1. What is the purpose of carrying out an inferential statistical test of experimental data?

2. What is the distinction between parametric and non-parametric tests?

Section 3

Other summative techniques

In this section some other (non-experimental) approaches to summative evaluation are discussed. These include usability audits, surveys and critical incident reporting.

Usability audits

Audits involve the checking of various aspects of the completed design against certain criteria. Audit instruments are often paper-based checklists (although some are now available as software packages), which list the various criteria, together with response categories for each item. Response categories, at their simplest, require a simple yes or no, pass or fail response, depending on whether that feature meets the criterion level. Most audit instruments use a range of response categories types that allow the person carrying out the audit to exercise their expert judgement. These might include rating scales or percentage scores.

Audit instruments are derived from guidelines or from in-house style guides (see Chapter 3) and have a close relationship with the setting of usability goals, discussed in Chapter 6. Typically, they use several categories to do with aspects of the user interface, e.g.:

- consistency of screen layout;
- navigation;
- error handling and help provision;
- consistent and appropriate use of colour.

Within each category, there are multiple specific questions. In this way, the audit can produce scores for each category and for the usability of the application as a whole. If formative evaluation has taken place throughout the development process, it should rarely be the case that major usability problems come to light as a consequence of carrying out an audit. If they do, of course, a decision needs to be made whether to delay the product launch and deal with the problem. More usually, the audit should demonstrate that the product has achieved predetermined benchmark values across all the major usability categories.

An example of a partial audit instrument might look like this:

Category: *screen layout*

Design feature	Criterion	Benchmark score	Obtained score
Location of 'exit' command buttons through application	Always at lower-right of screen	95%	95%
Sequence of menu items	Consistent functional groups	99%	98%
Default colour combination of screen banners	Always yellow on black	100%	100%
Font size for sub-headings	Always 14 point	100%	86%

The setting of benchmark values depends on an awareness of the relative importance of certain features, given that design almost always involves compromises and trade-offs. In the hypothetical example above, it may have been acknowledged earlier in the design process that the location of exit buttons should be at the lower-right of each screen if possible but that, in certain instances, it is not desirable or possible to effect this. The obtained measure corresponds to the criterion value for acceptability, so there is no problem here. However, the font size feature has clearly failed to achieve the criterion level and a decision needs to be made whether to deal with this problem.

Surveys

Another approach to summative evaluation is to use a survey instrument to collect the opinions and attitudes of potential users of an application. This method allows relatively large numbers of subjects exposure to a final prototype or beta version of a product and information is collected using a standardised questionnaire.

Post-release critical incident reporting

Useful information can be collected even when the product is released onto the market. Customer feedback or complaints, collected via a support desk system, can indicate usability problems that remained hidden even up to the point of product release. If this occurs, then a decision can be made whether to effect an immediate solution; or, if the problem is less serious, the customer feedback can contribute to the design of the next version of the product.

Quick test

1. What is the aim of carrying out a usability audit?
2. What information can critical incident reporting provide?

Section 4

End of chapter assessment

Questions

1. For what purposes would you employ a controlled product test to evaluate a user interface design?
2. A team has designed a web application promoting a small business. On the basis of earlier evaluation work and other information it is widely believed that the new product is an excellent application in terms of its usability and in other ways and that the application will meet the clients' requirements once the product is launched. You have been asked to design a controlled product test in order compare the new product with the hypothetical current market leader, identified as CML. The CML embodies much the same functionality as the product to be tested.

   Present an explanation of the experimental design and procedure under these headings:

   - **experimental design** (including a statement of the hypotheses to be tested and an explanation of the independent and dependent variables);
   - **participants** (or 'subjects' or 'users' or other suitable heading);
   - **equipment and rooms**;
   - **procedure** (exactly how it is proposed to conduct the test – in effect, a script).

3. Explain how usability audits are constructed and used.

Approach to answers

1. The aim of the test is twofold: (a) to provide the clients with evidence they can use in 'marketing' the product, in terms, for example, that the product is excellently designed (is highly 'usable' compared with other products, specifically the market leader available); and (b) to identify any weaknesses that it would be wise to remedy before the product is launched.

2. This question has many possible acceptable answers. The purpose is to get you to think what are likely to be the key independent variables and hypotheses within this scenario. Dependent variables will largely relate to the time taken to perform specific tasks and numbers and types of errors made by subjects. Some discussion needs to relate to numbers and categories of subjects and to the instructions they are given. A representative range of tasks needs to be defined.

3. Usability audits are constructed using relevant user interface guidelines, filtered through the experience of the design team. Categories are constructed and individual features listed within them. Benchmark values are set. The evaluators then assess the design giving observed scores in each category.

Section 5

Further reading and research

Further reading

Books and papers

Dix, A. *et al.* (1998) – Chapter 11 'Evaluation techniques'.

Newman, W. M. and Lamming, M. G. (1995) – Chapter 10 'Experiments in support of design'.

Nielsen, J. (1993) – Chapter 6 'Usability testing' and Chapter 7 'Usability assessment methods beyond testing'.

Nielsen, J. and Mack, R. L. (1994) – Chapter 8 (by Clare-Marie Karat) 'A comparison of user interface evaluation methods'.

Preece, J. *et al.* (2002) – Chapter 14 'Testing and modelling users'.

Websites

Microsoft. *http://www.microsoft.com/windows2000/professional/evaluation/news/air.asp* 'Comparative usability study of the Microsoft Windows operating systems' (author unknown) – a useful, if brief, example of how to write up an evaluation.

Research Methods Knowledge Base. *http://trochim.human.cornell.edu/kb* Comprehensive information and links about research methods. Compiled by Professor William Trochim, Cornell University.

Usability Methods Toolbox *http://jthom.best.vwh.net/usability/usable.htm* A summary of usability evaluation methods and techniques. Compiled by James Hom, as part of an MSc project at San José State University.

Further research

1. To develop further understanding of experimental design and statistical analysis it is useful to study journal articles reporting experimental results. There are numerous examples in the literature, for example Sears *et al.* (2001); Wolfson and Case (2000).

Chapter 8
Supporting the user: help and documentation

Chapter summary

The chapter starts by considering why users might need help, identifies the main categories of help, looks at some of the problems associated with the design of user assistance and identifies some common principles underpinning good quality user support. The next section looks at the characteristics of specific implementations of help, such as manuals, command prompts and so on. Finally, it outlines some general considerations when designing help, such as how to present it, and introduces the concept of the minimalist philosophy of documentation as opposed to more 'conventional' approaches.

Learning outcomes

Outcome 1: Understand some of the problems associated with help systems in the context of users' needs and be aware of design principles that support good quality support.
Question 1 at the end of the chapter gives you the opportunity to relate these ideas.

Outcome 2: Be able to explain the different ways that help systems can be implemented.
Question 2 at the end of the chapter tests your knowledge of the characteristics of different implementations of user support.

Outcome 3: Be aware of other issues relating to the design of user support including different styles of approach.
Question 3 at the end of the chapter tests your ability to distinguish between different modes of approach.

How will you be assessed on this?

In your practical work you would be expected to demonstrate that you had given some thought as to how to support the user of any software, or other products, that you have designed and implemented. At the very least, you should demonstrate that you can produce an effective (and evaluated) installation guide for example. You should demonstrate an awareness of help issues throughout the whole design process, for example by noting any particular difficulties experienced by users during evaluation exercises. You might be asked to design and implement some kind of help system as a project topic in its own right.

Examination questions would probably focus on:

- problems and difficulties associated with accessing and using help facilities;
- principles and guidelines to support the design of good quality support;
- the characteristics of different types of help;
- different approaches to designing support and learning materials.

Section 1

Introduction to user support

In this section we will consider why, and in what areas, users might need support; identify the main categories of support; look at some of the problems associated with the design of user assistance; identify some common principles underpinning good quality user support.

Even systems that have been well designed and evaluated will need to provide additional information to the user in the form of some sort of help and/or other support. High quality support helps the user learn to use a product quickly and effectively, correct errors and discover how to use more advanced functions. Research cited by Preece *et al.* (1994) suggests that users' typical concerns are in areas such as:

- goal exploration – what can I do with this software?
- definition and description – what does this do? what is that for?
- task achievement – how do I do such and such?
- diagnostic – how/why did that happen? how can I fix it?
- state identification – whereabouts am I?

Dix *et al.* (1998) further point out that users require various types of help at different times for particular purposes, and identify four main categories as outlined below. Particular implementations of assistance, which we will be looking at in the next section, fall into one of these general categories.

- **Quick reference.** Essentially a reminder for tools/commands that have been used before, for example particular command syntax.

- **Task-specific help.** Generally designed to provide additional assistance with performing a **particular** task at the time it is being performed.

- **Full explanation.** Provides a very detailed explanation of a particular tool or command that would be of interest to an experienced or curious user.

- **Tutorial.** A step-by-step guide, often illustrating precisely how a particular task can be performed – this would probably be aimed at new users of a system.

CRUCIAL TIP

There is a distinction between technical documentation and what might be called learning guides. Technical documentation, or reference, is more likely to contain information of value to the experienced user of a product and might act as an aide-memoire; learning guides tend to the 'how to'. For example, if you wanted to learn how to build web pages in HTML, it is unlikely that you would **initially** consult a list of HTML tags and their attributes; later on though you would wish to use such a list for reference to remind yourself of, perhaps, the syntax or the particular attributes supported by different browsers and so on. In this chapter the terms help, assistance, documentation and support are used more or less interchangeably.

Common difficulties

Although, as we will see, there are many different types of user assistance, it is useful to think about the problems that are common to many of them; some of these difficulties are outlined below.

Volume of material

Many systems nowadays are highly complex and so, in theory, sometimes require a hefty amount of documentation and help. Exceptions might be, for example, public access systems such as ticket machines that people want to use very quickly for specific and limited tasks.

Navigation difficulties

In view of the volume of data, often in the form of text-based content, it is not surprising that it can be easy to get lost or not be able to find information in a poorly designed help system. Paradoxically perhaps, a help system needs its own interface, which means that the material should be presented, structured and labelled effectively (information architecture).

Focus not on users' real tasks

Some user guides tend to be more of a technical reference manual or focus on the features of a product, rather than showing users how to accomplish particular tasks.

Poor error information

According to Lazonder and van der Meij (1995) novice users can typically spend 25-50% of their time making and trying to recover from errors. Ideally, error messages should appear at the appropriate time, describe what has actually occurred and why, then offer a sensible solution; unfortunately, in many cases they are not implemented in such a way as to be of any use at all. Thimbleby *et al.* (2002) describe a railway ticket machine that informs the user that a ticket cannot be printed (because it has run out of paper) **after** someone may have spent a considerable amount of time trying to select the correct ticket.

Poor writing style

When the help button is pressed on the ticket machine mentioned above, in certain states, it displays the message 'Help not implemented for ContextID 0011' – clearly more meaningful to the programmer than the user. Apart from avoiding technical jargon, it is important that the writing style is clear, consistent, and free from spelling and grammatical errors. Terminology is important, the User Interface Engineering company have even suggested (2000) that users might prefer words such as 'tips' or 'hints' over 'help', which some people might construe as an admission of failure.

Help/documentation added as afterthought

Help is often added as an afterthought, sometimes by persons who are perhaps not best qualified to do so, since it can require specialist skills to produce effective support systems. Ideally, help systems should be developed throughout the whole design process.

Poor product design

Thimbleby and Addison (1996) observe that many products are badly designed in the first place, in particular by being unnecessarily complex; they hold that flawed and complex design is then inevitably reflected in the product's documentation.

CRUCIAL TIP

When conducting evaluation it is possible to start identifying areas where users may need **particular** help.

Identifying principles

It follows, from what you have been reading, that help systems have to be designed carefully in order to provide appropriate support. Just as a system in its entirety is more effective if it accords with certain design principles (see Chapter 3), so it is with help. Again, Dix *et al.* (1998) identify particular principles which supply useful benchmarks:

Availability

Help should be available whenever it is required, ideally without exiting from the particular task that the user is engaged in. It would be even more frustrating if the user had to close down the application and open another to obtain assistance.

Accuracy and completeness

It is probably best to make the assumption that people may need assistance with any task and so, ideally, the **whole** system should be supported; however, as mentioned earlier, evaluation processes may reveal particular areas of concern. Obviously, care must be taken to ensure that the help offered is precise and accurate.

Consistency

Help should be consistent both **within** the different media that might be provided (for example the online help system and the paper manual) and **across** different delivery mechanisms; in other words an online system should offer the same content, style and presentation. It is worth noting that this principle can sometimes be difficult to maintain across different releases of a product.

Robustness

Robustness is an important design principle for the whole system; it should not behave in unexpected ways or even worse, actually crash. Help (as part of the user interface) should clearly conform to the same principle and be designed to provide clear error handling and predictable performance.

Flexibility

We have already noted that users have different needs hence help systems should reflect this concept. For example, support can be offered at different levels of complexity that allow the user to progressively drill down through various levels of information.

Unobtrusiveness

Help should normally be supplied when it is specifically requested by the user and not intrude on the task they are engaged in. Neither should help interfere with the system itself, for example by slowing it down or masking parts of the screen.

CRUCIAL CONCEPT

Users need **appropriate support** depending on their level of expertise and what tasks they are trying to accomplish. Generally, users share a typical set of concerns. There are common difficulties and problems associated with the implementation of user support. Good quality help systems share common design principles.

Quick test

1. What concerns do users typically have when learning to use a new system?

2. What are the main categories of help systems?

3. What are the problems associated with help systems?

4. List the important design principles that particularly apply to the design of help systems.

Section 2

Different implementations of user support

The previous section outlined four main categories of user help. In this section we will be examining the characteristics of specific implementations of online, paper and other forms of support.

Command assistance

This is a relatively simple approach in one sense. It provides, on demand, further information on a particular **command** and is therefore commonly to be found in non-windowed applications such as operating systems like DOS or UNIX. As an example, if you wanted to copy a file from one location to another using DOS, you may remember that the particular command is 'copy' but forget the exact syntax. To find out more about the command, you could type in 'copy /?' (and press return) whereupon the system would return a screen outlining the syntax of that particular command and its various switches. You will hopefully have realised that are several problems evident however simple this approach seems to be. The first is the assumption that the user knows what the command is in the first place (i.e. 'copy'). Secondly, and perhaps more importantly, it assumes an even deeper knowledge of the whole concept of files, directories and so on. Finally, it will probably violate an important principle: depending on the amount of text the system outputs to explain a particular command, what was typed earlier may now have disappeared off the screen.

CRUCIAL TIP

Try the above for yourself, since you may not be familiar with command line interfaces. You may need to use your system's help to find out how to open a 'DOS box' in the first place – how useful was it?

Command prompts

Sometimes a system will provide help if a command (such as DOS 'copy' mentioned earlier) is incorrectly entered for some reason. For example, the user may have specified a file to copy that didn't exist, or used incorrect syntax. Often, an error message is output, which may or may not provide guidance on how to resolve the error. Again, you **might** wish to try this for yourself on your own system although if you are a novice user you may find it rather daunting and be worried that you will delete or move an important file!

Context sensitive help

This is sometimes referred to as 'field level help'. It is designed so that help is generally provided at the user's request and is specific to the task in hand. It might be invoked by, for example:

- hitting a dedicated function key, such as 'F1';
- clicking the right-hand mouse button;
- pressing a 'help button' provided on the screen;
- resting the cursor over an icon ('tool tips'; 'balloons').

There is some evidence (Grayling, 1998) to suggest that users prefer context-sensitive help to other approaches such as menu-based help systems. This is probably because it is relatively unobtrusive and does not interrupt the flow of work.

Online tutorials

These tend to fall into several variants. **Interactive** tutorials lead the user step by step to help them complete a real task, whereas **non-interactive** implementations are often animations that merely illustrate how to do something. Other forms could be termed **partially-interactive**; a 'real' interface may be provided, but one that supports only partial functionality – for example, many of the demonstration systems provided by online banking systems. More traditional tutorials, in the form of self-test questionnaires, lend themselves to an online approach.

Online documentation

Whether implemented within the application itself, or via the internet, or sometimes as a mixture of both, this method offers a number of advantages over, say, paper manuals. In theory at least, online documentation is constantly available and is always up to date. By contrast, it lacks the portability of paper and, perhaps more importantly, is easy to implement poorly. Hypertext/hypermedia is often the technique used to build help systems, so all the desirable guidelines that relate to other hypertext type systems (such as web pages) should be applied; for example, supplying navigational aids, history lists and so on.

CRUCIAL TIP

Hypertext, hypermedia and multimedia are often used interchangeably – you should understand the difference between these terms. Hypertext is a way of arranging non-sequential text-based information in blocks such that it can be accessed from different starting points – the blocks are referred to as **nodes**. Within each node there are one or more **anchors**, which are specific locations within the node; anchors **link** to other anchors either within the same node or to anchors in other nodes – in this way the reader can jump to other sections (nodes) of a hypertext document. **Hypermedia** essentially works in exactly the same way, the difference being that the information is contained within more than one medium, for example text and animations, i.e. **multimedia**.

Intelligent help

Intelligent help attempts to monitor and respond to the activities of the user and usually incorporates (or builds) intrinsic models of the user, the task and the domain. Various degrees of adaptability can be embodied:

- a **non-adaptive** system (possibly produced by a domain expert or interface designer etc.) may incorporate a model of a 'typical' user and assumes that users are similar;
- an **adaptable** system may be modified by the user and can be as simple as maintaining user profiles; here the onus is on the user to make modifications to the system;
- an **adaptive** system responds to the behaviour of the user then builds and refines a model (perhaps based on an initial default).

The implementation of intelligent help can include features such as:

- using various heuristics, e.g. 'IF user delays for >10 seconds THEN prompt with command';
- 'learning' users' preferences e.g. changing defaults automatically;
- comparing users' behaviour with optimal set of actions then prompting towards correct actions;
- anticipation of errors and helping the user to avoid or recover from the error.

Building in intelligence obviously introduces additional challenges that are, in part, concerned with the difficulties associated with interpreting user behaviour in context. I am fairly confident that you have all encountered the 'helpful' assistant that often pops up at inappropriate moments, incorporated into a certain popular word processing package!

Paper manuals

According to many sources (Rettig 1991; Lazonder and van der Meij, 1993 etc.) users seldom read manuals; it appears that that they are only consulted as a last resort, when the trial and error approach has failed. Nielsen (1993) further suggests that manual consultation occurs at the point when people are in a state of some alarm and require immediate assistance. One might then question why practically all software comes equipped with at least one stout, shrink-wrapped volume since the paper manual appear to be such anathema. Clearly, manuals can suffer from all the problems (outlined in Section 1) that are common to all forms of user support, i.e.:

- volume of material;
- navigational difficulties;
- focus not on users' real tasks;
- poor error information;
- poor writing style;
- poor product design.

Despite their propensity for mediocre quality, paper manuals nonetheless offer other more positive affordances such as: relative portability; uncomplicated browsing; easy to make notes in; physical bookmarking and so on. And so the paper manual will remain with us, and it is the responsibility of whoever designs them to exploit their more positive characteristics and deal with potential problems.

─── CRUCIAL TIP ───

Affordance, in essence, means the perceived properties of something that suggest how it could be interacted with. For example, the shape of a car steering wheel implies that it could be turned.

General support

In addition to the resources outlined above, users can obtain assistance from a variety of other sources. Many people derive benefit from, for example, face-to-face training, although this can be constrained by the quality of the documentation provided and the skills of the particular instructor. Another common and very effective method of learning is to watch and/or ask questions of colleagues. Many products are supported by helpdesks or telephone hotlines, which – as you are probably acutely aware – unfortunately vary widely in terms of their actual helpfulness; a frequent response to questions is to advise the enquirer to 'read the manual'. Increasing use is being made of product support websites that often include FAQs (frequently asked questions), downloads of patches/upgrades, and email facilitated help and so on.

Some products will provide a whole range of support incorporating some or all of the methods outlined above, which introduces yet another challenge: how to keep all of this support in synchronisation?

─── CRUCIAL CONCEPT───

There are many different techniques for implementing **help**; they vary in their level of complexity and effectiveness. In common with all techniques, each has associated benefits and 'costs'. Specialist skill and knowledge may be required to select and implement appropriate forms of support.

Quick test

Outline the different implementations of user help.

Section 3

Designing user support

In the preceding sections you have seen that users have particular needs according to their level of skill and the context of their particular concerns. You will also be aware of the many problems associated with providing help but recognise that adherence to certain design principles can inform the design of user support in all its many forms. In this section we will look at some general considerations when designing help and also introduce the concept of the minimalist approach to user instruction.

When should help be designed?

It has already been mentioned that the design of support and assistance should be integral to the overall design process and not merely tacked on after the main implementation. There are several junctures during the design effort at which help requirements can be revealed and accommodated: task and user analysis, for example, can help identify and model support needs at each point of interaction; evaluation exercises often elicit particular areas of difficulty.

How could help be requested?

A quick review of Section 2 should indicate the range of choices available, for instance, the user could be provided with help by an intelligent system, in which case summoning assistance is to some extent taken out of their control. Other options could include:

- typing in a command;
- pressing a particular function key;
- clicking a help button;
- opening a paper manual.

How could help be displayed on the screen?

Again, there exist a whole range of possibilities, for example:

- in a new window;
- in a pop-up box;
- filling the existing window;
- in a split screen;
- floating;
- as a hint (e.g. tool tips, balloons);
- visual cues (e.g. changes to font, size, colour, format).

Who should design user support?

Interface designers or programmers are not necessarily the most appropriate individuals to design and implement user support. Increasingly, help specialists are being deployed who are 'descended' from the technical authors who used to be responsible just for writing paper manuals.

The minimalist approach to designing user support

There are numerous references (Carroll, 1984, 1990; Carroll *et al.*, 1987, Lazonder and van der Meij, 1995; van der Meij and Carroll, 1995: van der Meij, 1992 etc.) to the minimalist philosophy of documentation design. Originally envisaged as an approach to designing paper-based manuals, the essential principles can be applied to the design of any type of user support or learning materials.

The emphasis of the minimalist approach can be categorised under three main principles: readability, learnability and navigation support – these were identified by Mayhew (1992) as being supportive of good quality user support. Table 8.1 below expands the minimalist concepts in more detail by fleshing out the principles with indicative guidelines.

Table 8.1 Principles of minimalist approach to documentation

Readability (text optimisation)	Learnability (learning by doing)	Navigation support
write in short, simple sentences	novices expect to succeed by exploring, reading and thinking	history lists
use active tense	allow users to start immediately on meaningful tasks	bookmarks
avoid jargon	new material should be based on users' prior knowledge	index
don't 'spell out' everything	use analogy, examples and illustrations	site map
omit prefaces, introductions etc.	error recognition and recovery emphasis	'on the spot information' related to task in hand
keep chapters short and self-contained	safe to explore	table of contents
Make references implicit by describing prerequisite **goals** (rather than repeating information elaborated elsewhere)	guided exploration	break down chapters into tasks and sub-tasks so that irrelevant material can be skipped

An example provided by Herajarvi (1998) demonstrates how minimalist instruction and 'conventional' instruction might be written, and is shown in Table 8.2. It relates to a user guide for some medical patient record software; the left-hand column presents an example of minimalist instruction of how to produce a prescription note, the right-hand column shows the more conventional type of instruction to do the same task.

Criticisms of the minimalist approach (e.g. Draper, 1998) typically raise the following issues:

- lack of explicit guidelines;
- assumption that people **want to learn** (as opposed to just completing a task);
- lack of fundamental explanation which may allow the reader to place concerns in context and facilitate prediction;
- contradicts conventional wisdom concerning good writing style, e.g. providing a preview to prime the reader about the main points to look out for;
- some systems, for example those of a safety critical nature, need more comprehensive instruction and explanation.

We could conclude this chapter by reflecting that the choice of user support and its mode of implementation probably depend on the type of software, the purpose of the documentation, the characteristics of the users and the context of their tasks. Help forms part of the user interface, and as such can be evaluated as to its effectiveness using some of the techniques described in Chapters 6 and 7.

Table 8.2 Minimalist *v* conventional instruction

Minimalist	Convential
Writing a prescription You can either renew the old prescription or write a new prescription.	**How to write a prescription** A prescription can be created by renewing an old prescription or writing a new one.
1. Choose the **Create new** button. 2. Fill in the details of the prescription. 3. To print the prescription, choose the **Print** button. 4. To save and file the prescription, choose the **OK** button. The prescription is filed in the patient record and a new link is added to the record text. *If you get a confirmation message when choosing the OK button, you have not printed the prescription yet. Print first and then choose OK.* *On your own: using phrases in prescriptions* You can use ready-made phrases when writing a prescription by choosing the **Find phrase**...option from **Edit** menu. Try them and see.	1. Choose the **Create new** button. If there is no old prescription open, a new prescription is created on an empty window. Patient's name and date of birth will appear automatically on top of the screen. Also the date and place will appear on the bottom of the screen according to user information. 2. Fill in the details of the prescription. You can either use only the first of the two fields or both. If the second field is left blank, printing will mark it as used, by filling it with Z characters. You can also use ready-made phrases when writing prescriptions. 3. To print the prescription, choose the **Print** button. Change the print options, if you wish, and choose **OK** button. 4. To save and file the prescription, choose the **OK** button. The prescription is filed in the patient record and a new link is added to the record text. **Please note:** The prescription must be printed before saving and filing. This is to ensure that a particular prescription is delivered only once. After saving, printing is no longer available. The system will prompt you for that.

--- CRUCIAL CONCEPT ---

When **designing user support**, decisions have to be made as to when to design it, how to invoke and display it, and who should prepare any documentation. Depending on the audience and the context of use, one could opt for either a minimalist or a conventional approach. Help needs to be evaluated as part of the user interface.

Quick test

1. Describe some of the issues involved in designing user support.

2. What are the main principles associated with the minimalist approach?

Section 4

End of chapter assessment

Questions

1. Identify the difficulties that users have in connection with using support systems and suggest the main design principles that, if adhered to, help to ensure good quality support.

2. Identify and **explain five** main implementations of user support.

3. Outline the benefits and disadvantages of the minimalist approach to user support.

Approach to answers

1. You might start by explaining that whether implemented in an electronic or paper medium, all support systems share common difficulties (outline them). Continue by explaining the particular problems, e.g. volume of material and so on perhaps (relating your points to different media). Rather than simply listing the design principles, you could attempt to relate them to the problems, e.g. 'It could be argued that online help is more easily **available** than paper-based help...' etc.

2. It would not be enough simply to make a list, e.g.

   - command prompts;
   - intelligent/adaptive help;
   - context sensitive help;
     etc.

   The key word in the question is 'explain', so you would need to describe the different types of help in some detail, giving illustrative examples, and also make some distinctions between them, for example by considering the extent to which the different types address users' concerns.

3. You could start by identifying the main guidelines (e.g. write in short, simple sentences etc.) and explain how they support the underlying desirable principles (e.g. readability etc.). Then you could address some of the criticisms of the approach (e.g. the assumption that everyone wants to learn as opposed to completing a task etc.). If you have conducted further personal research along the lines suggested in the section Further Research you may have your own observations to add, but beware of writing this up in anecdotal style and relying too much on it as evidence.

Section 5

Further reading and research

Further reading

Books and papers

Dix, A. *et al.* (1998) – Chapter 12 'Help and documentation'.
Grayling, T. (1998).
Nielsen, J. (1993) –Section 5.10 'Help and documentation'.
Preece, J. *et al.* (1994) – Chapter 15 'User support and online information'.

Shneiderman, B. (1998) – Chapter 12 'Printed manuals, online help and tutorials'.
Thimbleby, H. and Addison, M. (1996).

Websites

Institute of Scientific and Technical Communicators. *http://www.istc.org.uk* (last accessed
24/11/02). 'The largest UK body representing professionals, communicators and information designers.' See especially 'Using BS 7830' (Guide to the design and preparation
of on-screen documentation for users of application software) on the Standards page
at *http://www.istc.org.uk/site/bs7830.asp* (last accessed 24/11/02).

Society for Technical Communication. *http://www.techcomm-online.org* (last accessed
24/11/02). Archive of the journal *Technical Communication* – many of the older
papers are available for download as full text.

Further research

1. Review Section 1, in particular the main categories of help as identified by Dix *et al.*
(1998). Review Section 2, which outlines how different types of user support can be
implemented.

   Draw a grid along the lines of the one shown below in Table 8.3 with the main
categories of help as column headers. Then complete the grid by placing the different
types of user support under appropriate headings; 'online tutorials' has already been
placed into Table 8.3 to get you started.

Table 8.3 A classification of user support

Quick reference	Task specific help	Full explanation	Tutorial
			online tutorials

   When you have done this, consider to what extent the different types of help offer
assistance in connection with the user concerns identified by Preece *et al.* (1994) and
outlined in Section 1. You might want to annotate your grid to record your thoughts.

2. You have probably produced more than one piece of software either as part of your
studies or, perhaps, in connection with your job. Did you design and produce any user
guidance, for example some installation instructions?

   Select one of your pieces of software and produce **two** sets of installation instructions, one in a 'conventional' style and one in a 'minimalist' style. Now ask two people
who have not used your software before to install it; one person should use the
conventional instructions and the other should use the minimalist instructions.
Observe your subjects while they are carrying out the process and note down: how
long it took them to complete it; what errors were made and if/how they were
recovered from; any verbal comments; any non-verbal behaviour. You could also
interview the people afterwards. What conclusions, if any, could you make about the
different styles of instruction?

Appendix
Examination questions and approach to answers

1. (a) Outline the **scope** of designing the user interface, giving specific examples where appropriate.
   (b) Many organisations invest a great deal of money in IT systems. It is increasingly recognised that there are tangible benefits associated with ensuring that systems are well engineered in terms of affording good usability.
   Identify and explain **five** such benefits that well engineered systems might provide to an organisation.

2. (a) Describe, in detail, any **one** model of user involvement in the user interface design process.
   (b) Discuss the benefits and problems associated with involving users in the user interface design process, drawing on evidence from the academic literature and other relevant sources.

3. (a) Explain the meaning of, and differentiate between, principles, guidelines and standards in the context of user interface design, illustrating your answer as appropriate.
   (b) It has been observed that software designers sometimes ignore, or make limited use of in-house guidelines.
   (i) Discuss the reasons why this might occur.
   (ii) Put forward arguments (targeted at software designers) illustrating the benefits of using guidelines.

4. (a) Describe any **three** techniques for eliciting and analysing the user requirements at the outset of the user interface development process.
   (b) For **each** of the three techniques you have identified in part (a) above:

   (i) Explain whether the information obtained would be primarily qualitative or quantitative.
   (ii) Illustrate, using examples, how the information obtained could identify design and/or usability issues that would have to be addressed.

5. Imagine that you wish to listen to some music (recorded on a CD-ROM) at home: Using the hierarchical task analysis procedure, model the tasks involved to achieve your goal.

6. (a) Explain what is meant by KLM.
   (b) Illustrate the use of KLM by decomposing (using the appropriate operators) the task of using a text editor such as MS Word to move a piece of text from one location to another.

7. (a) Explain the principal issues that need to be taken into account when developing an evaluation plan.
   (b) Discuss the benefits and disadvantages of using field trials as an evaluation technique.

8. Suggest an appropriate medium for an in-house web style guide, supporting your answer with a rationale for the choice of medium.

Approach to Answers

An approach to answering the above questions is given below.

1. (a) Answers could include:

   - design of input and output devices (e.g. keyboards, mice);
   - design of workstation environment (i.e. ergonomic factors);
   - range of tasks supported (e.g. task specific such as Sage accounting software or generic such as MS Excel);
   - the user/s (i.e. taking into account the user's characteristics and range of senses);
   - information layout and meaning (e.g. how appropriate layout of text in a report can enhance seek times for specific information, distinguishing between input fields and labels in online forms).

   A basic pass mark might be achieved by simply listing these items, but you would need to provide further explanation than is shown here to get a higher mark.

   (b) General business benefits would include **efficiency, effectiveness, productivity, safety and user** satisfaction. Specific benefits (as identified by NatWest Usability Services):

   - improved image to users;
   - higher quality end product;
   - lower costs over life of product;
   - lower initial/on-going training costs;
   - improved user efficiency/accuracy;
   - lower help-desk costs.

   Again, this simple list needs to be enhanced by further description/explanation to achieve good marks. You would need, for example to explain what was meant by 'efficiency'.

2. (a) There are numerous choices here, for example Brun-Cottan and Wall's user-centred process model, Axtell *et al.*'s user-involvement method etc. Obviously this question lends itself to a diagrammatic answer, but you should always supplement any visual illustrations with explanatory text. A common mistake here is to see the word 'model' in the question and write about general process models such as the waterfall model, the star model etc.

   (b) You would be likely to include ideas such as:

   Benefits – Evidence that direct links between end-users and developers results in more successful products (Keil and Carmel 1995).

   - users play an active role throughout the analysis and design processes;
   - designer and users jointly evaluate the usability of a proposed design as early as possible; design can be modified as part of iterative process;
   - likely to result in more usable product;
   - greater feeling of 'ownership' of system;
   - not necessarily time-consuming, with use of quick prototyping approaches.

   Problems – no single model for doing this (although JAD starting to emerge as a *de facto* standard. Evidence from e.g. Heinbokel *et al.* (1996) that user involvement causes problems, such as:

   - lack of innovation;
   - managers may be reluctant to authorise time to release users;
   - 'surrogates' or other intermediaries may be substituted for users;
   - users may become too involved and identify with the designer/s;
   - perceived as time consuming and disruptive.

   Note: although bullet points are useful for getting ideas down quickly, you should expand on them wherever possible.

115

3. (a) Your answer could be along the lines of:

Design principle – a widely-accepted goal or 'truth', often to do with some aspect of human cognition with respect to interaction with computer systems, and often derived from some body of theory. Examples: consistency, flexibility, reversibility etc. General and widely applicable. Underpin guidelines and standards.

Design guideline: a hint, tip, or recommendation, sometimes theoretically-derived, but often emerging from practitioner experience. Couched in more imperative terms.

Examples: e.g. 'always use F1 to invoke help'.

Standard: you should distinguish generally between *de jure*, *de facto* and proprietary standards. Give examples: ISO 9241 (*de jure*); MS Windows (*de facto*) and so on.

(b) (i) Could include:

Problems – tend to be either too general or too implementation-specific; difficulties for designers in interpretation, prioritisation of guidelines. Need meta-guidelines about how to make trade-off decisions regarding use of guidelines. May be inaccessible, poorly presented. May be contradictory or ambiguous. Designers may perceive that guidelines constrain innovation.

Other sensible and relevant points would receive credit; for example you could link this question to the general problems associated with all types of guidance such as printed manuals etc.

(ii) Could include points such as:
Benefits – use of guidelines, to an extent, ensures a degree of consistency within and between designs; reduces likelihood of significant design flaws; forms the basis of future standardisation activities. Designers don't have to 'reinvent the wheel' – e.g. internet/intranet designers would not have to design from scratch page templates etc.

4. (a) Could include: structured/unstructured interviews, focus groups, surveys and questionnaires, prototyping, task analysis, observation and so on. You would probably get a few marks for simply identifying techniques and listing them, but high marks would require a good level of explanation.

(b) (i) It **could** be argued that any technique has the propensity to provide primarily qualitative or quantitative data, or even a mixture of the two. Sensible, well-argued and supported points should receive credit.

(ii) Examples:

- (from interviews) user could explain why current systems difficult to use;
- (from task analysis) a simpler task structure with fewer actions could achieve the same goal;
- (from focus group) users could express a strong dislike of a particular colour combination.

Obviously, you would need to expand these points substantially.

5. You could use the approach as illustrated below, this follows the notation used in JSP (Jackson Structured Programming) although there are other appropriate notations.

Your answer would not necessarily look exactly like this since there are various ways of decomposing the problem. Also, if you decided to play a CD on your PC some of the discrete actions would be different anyway. A common mistake is to draw the diagram the wrong way up (i.e. with actions at the top and the super-ordinate task at the bottom) so that it is in fact a flowchart rather than an HTA diagram.

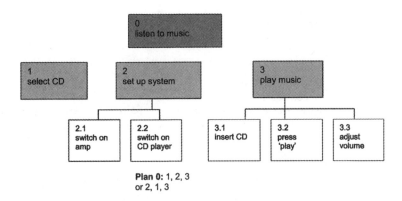

Plan 0: 1, 2, 3
or 2, 1, 3

6. (a) Your answer would probably read something like this:

'The keystroke level model is a variant of GOMS (goals operators methods selection rules) used to make detailed predictions about user performance. There are generally seven operators: five physical, one mental and one system:
K striking keys; B clicking mouse button; P pointing mouse at target; H switching hand from mouse to keyboard; D drawing lines using the mouse; M mentally preparing to perform action; R system response.'

(b) This is one way of decomposing the task, though there could be other ways of achieving the same objective.

'To move a string of text from one location to another **could** involve: mental preparation, moving the hand to mouse, positioning the cursor on the first character, clicking mouse button, dragging cursor to end of string, releasing mouse button, striking 'Ctrl' and 'X', moving cursor to new text position, striking 'Ctrl' and 'V', waiting for system response.'

Represented as:

mental preparation	M
move hand to mouse	H
position cursor at start of string	P
click mouse button	B
drag cursor to end of string	H
release mouse button	B
strike 'Ctrl' and 'X'	KK
reposition cursor	P
strike 'Ctrl' and 'V'	KK
await system response	R

Additionally, you could then show the decomposition as a formula, i.e.:

$$T = 4t_K + 2t_B + 2t_P + 2t_H + 0_D + 1t_M + 1t_R$$

7. (a) You would need to include:

- requirement to relate technique/tool to stage of product development (i.e. formative or summative technique);
- key issues:

  usability and other design goals
  need to be clear, specific and measurable;
  especially for summative evaluation to be effective;

techniques
multiple? (convergent validity);
resources;
timescales;
logistical considerations;
ethical considerations;
evaluation team?
interface designers;
users;
UI specialists/experts.

Again, you would need to expand on these bullet points

(b) Some topics to include in your discussion could include:

Useful for:

interacting with users;
getting ideas for new versions;

conducted in users' environment
contextual (contextual validity);
evaluator can view system as part of total environment;

methods can include:
many of the 'laboratory' techniques;

problems
interruptions;
difficult to control;
considered 'unscientific'.

8. This should start with a discussion about **why** designers are sometimes reluctant to use guidelines e.g. difficult to access, constrain creativity etc.

    The most obvious choice might be an online hypertext-based medium for accessibility, ease of navigation and ease of maintenance. This could take the form of a CD-ROM or an intranet site for example.

    You could propose a paper medium for portability and usability.

    You might go further and suggest an intelligent help system that automatically checks systems for compliance with guidelines.

References

Abowd, G. D. and Beale, R. (1991). Users, systems and interfaces: a unifying framework for interaction. In D. Diaper and N. Hammond (Eds.) HCI 91: *People and Computers VI*. Cambridge University Press.

Alavi, M. (1984). An assessment of the prototyping approach to information systems development. *Communications of the ACM*, 27, (6), 556-563.

Allen, C.D. (1995). Succeeding as a clandestine change agent. *Communications of the ACM*, 38, (5), 81-86.

Axtell, C.M., Waterson, P.E. and Clegg, C.W. (1997). Problems integrating user participation into software development. *International Journal of Human-Computer Studies*, 47, 323-345.

Bærentsen, K.B. and Slavensky, H. (1999). A contribution to the design process. *Communications of the ACM*, 42, (5), 73-77.

Benyon, D.R. (1995). Whither the life cycle? Paper presented at an IEE Colloquium on 'Integrating HCI in the life cycle', Savoy Place, London, 11 April, 1995.

Beyer, H. and Holtzblatt, K. (1995). Apprenticing with the customer. *Communications of the ACM*, 38, (5), 45-52.

Beyer, H. and Holtzblatt, K. (1998). *Contextual Design: Defining Customer-Centred Systems*. Morgan Kaufmann Publishers, INC.

Bias, R. G. and Mayhew, D. J. (Eds.) (1994). *Cost Justifying Usability*. Academic Press.

Bødker, S. (1996). Creating conditions for participation: conflicts and resources in systems development. *Human-Computer Interaction*, 11, (3), 215-236.

Booth, P. (1989). *An Introduction to Human-Computer Interaction*. Lawrence Erlbaum.

Brown, J. and Duguid, P. (2000). *The Social Life of Information*. Harvard Business School Press.

Brun-Cottan, F. and Wall, P. (1995). Using video to re-present the user. *Communications of the ACM*, 38, (5), 61-71.

Buie, E. (1999). HCI standards: a mixed blessing. *Interactions*, March + April, 36-42.

Buzan, T. and Buzan, B. (2000). *The Mind Map Book*. BBC Consumer Publishing (Books).

Card, S.K., Moran, T.P., and Newell, A. (1983). *The Psychology of Human-Computer Interaction*. Lawrence Erlbaum Associates.

Carey, M.S., Stammers, R.B. and Astley, J.A. (1989). Human-computer interaction design: the potential and pitfalls of Hierarchical Task Analysis. In: D. Diaper (Ed.), *Task Analysis for Human-Computer Interaction*. Ellis Horwood Ltd, pp. 56-74.

Carroll, J.M. (1984) Minimalist training. *Datamation*, 30, 125-136.

Carroll, J.M. (1990). *The Nurnberg Funnel*. MIT Press.

Carroll, J.M., Mack, R.L., Robertson, S.P. and Rosson, M.B. (1994). Binding objects to scenarios of use. *International Journal of Human-Computer Interaction*, 41, 243-276.

Carroll, J. M., Smith-Kerker, P. L., Ford, J. R. and Masur-Rimetz, S. A. (1987). The minimal manual. *Human-Computer Interaction*, 3, 123-153.

Christie, B., Scane, R. and Collyer, J. (1995). Evaluation of human-computer interaction at the user interface to advanced IT systems. In J.R. Wilson and E. Nigel Corlett (Eds.) (1995) *Evaluation of Human Work: A Practical Ergonomics Methodology* (2nd edition). Taylor and Francis.

Clarke, D.T. and Crum, G.P. (1994). Dialogue specification and control: a review of models and techniques. *Information and Software Technology*, 36, (9), 539-547.

Concise Oxford Dictionary (1995). Ninth edition. Clarendon Press.

Cooper, A. (1999). *The Inmates are Running the Asylum*. SAMS, a Division of Macmillan Computer Publishing.

Cottrell, S. (1999). *The Study Skills Handbook*. Macmillan.

Damodaran, L. (1996). User involvement in the systems design process – a practical guide for users. *Behaviour and Information Technology*, 15, (6), 363-377.

Dawson, C. W. (2000). *The Essence of Computing Projects: A Student's Guide*. Prentice Hall.

Dix, A. J., Finlay, J. E., Abowd, G. D. and Beale, R. (1998). *Human Computer Interaction, 2nd edition*. Prentice Hall.

Draper, S.W. (1998). 'Practical problems and proposed solutions in designing action-centered documentation'. In J. M. Carroll (Ed.) *Minimalism Beyond the Nurnberg Funnel*. MIT Press.

Faulkner, X. (2000). *Usability Engineering*. Macmillan Press Ltd.

Foley, J.D. (1983). Managing the design of user-computer interfaces. *Computer Graphics World,* 12, 47-56.

Gardiner, M. and Christie, B. (Eds.) (1987). *Applying Cognitive Psychology to User-Interface Design*. John Wiley and Sons.

Gardner, J. (1999). Strengthening the focus on users' working practices. *Communications of the ACM*, 42, (5), 79-82.

Gerhardt-Powals, J. (1996). Cognitive engineering principles for enhancing human-computer performance. *International Journal of Human-Computer Interaction* 8, (2), 189-211.

Grayling, T. (1998). Fear and loathing of the help menu: a usability test of online help. *Technical Communication*, 45 (2), 168-179.

Greenberg, S. (1998). Prototyping for design and evaluation. *http://pages.cpsc.ucalgary.ca/~saul/681/1998/prototyping/survey.html* (last accessed 24/11/02).

Gugerty, L. (1993). The use of analytical models in human-computer interface design. *International Journal of Man-Machine Studies*, 38, 625-660.

Harel, D. (1988). On visual formalisms. *Communications of the ACM*, 31, (5), 514-530.

Hartson, H. R. and Hix, D. (1989). Toward empirically derived methodologies and tools for human-computer interface development. *International Journal of Man-Machine Studies*, 31, 477-494.

Heinbokel, T., Sonnentag, S., Frese, M., Stolte, W. and Brodbeck, F.C. (1996). Don't underestimate the problems of user centredness in software development projects - there are many! *Behaviour and Information Technology*, 15, (4), 226-236.

Herajarvi, M. (1998). Design Principles of User Documentation. Unpublished paper produced as part of MSc in User Interface Design, London Guildhall University.

Horrocks, I. (1999). *Constructing the User Interface with Statecharts*. Addison Wesley.

Hughes, M. (1999). Rigor in usability testing. *Technical Communication*, Fourth Quarter, 488-494.

Hutchings, A. F. and Knox, S.T. (1995). Creating products customers demand. *Communications of the ACM*, 38, (5), 72-80.

ISO 9241-11: 1998. Ergonomic requirements for office work with visual display terminals (VDTs) – Part II: Guidance on usability. International Organization for Standardization.

ISO 13407: 1999. Human-centred design processes for interactive systems. International Organization for Standardization.

Kaiser, P. K. *The Joy of Visual Perception: A Web Book. http://www.yorku.ca/eye.* (Site last visited 1/5/02).

Karat, J. (1988). Software Evaluation Methodologies. In M. Helander (Ed.) (1988) *Handbook of Human-Computer Interaction*. Elsevier Science Publishers B.V. (North-Holland).

Karat, J. (1994) A business case approach to usability cost justification. In R. G. Bias and D. J. Mayhew (Eds.). *Cost Justifying Usability*. Academic Press.

Keil, M. and Carmel, E. (1995). Customer-developer links in software development. *Communications of the ACM*, 38, (5), 33-44.

Knight, J. and Jefsioutine, M. (2002). Relating usability to design practice. In M. Maguire and K. Adeboye (Eds.) *Proceedings of the 1st European UPA Conference*. British Computer Society.

Kraut, R.E. and Streeter, L.A. (1995). Coordination in software development. *Communications of the ACM*, 38, (3), 69-81.

Lazonder, A. W. and van der Meij, H. (1993). The minimal manual: Is less really more? *International Journal of Man-Machine Studies*, 39 (5), 729-752.

Lazonder, A. W. and van der Meij, H. (1995). Error information in tutorial documentation: supporting users' errors to facilitate initial skill learning. *International Journal of Human-Computer Studies*, 42 (2), 185-206.

Löwgren, J. and Laurén, U. (1993). Supporting the use of guidelines and style guides in professional user interface design. *Interacting with Computers*, 5, (4), 385-396.

Lund, A.M. (1997). Another approach to cost justifying usability. *Interactions*, 4, (3), 48-56.

Lynch, P.J. and Horton, S. (1992). *Web Style Guide*, 2nd edition. Yale University Press.

Madsen, K.H. (1999). The diversity of usability practices. *Communications of the ACM*, 42, (5), 61-62.

Maguire, M. C. (incorporating material by Kirakowski, J. and Vereker, N.). *User-Centred Requirements Handbook*. Deliverable D5.1, Telematics Applications.

RESPECT project (TE2010). Version 2.21, April 1997. *http://www.ejeisa.com/nectar/ respect/5.3/contents.htm* (last accessed 24/11/02).

Maguire, M. C. (1999). A review of user interface design guidelines for public information kiosk systems. *International Journal of Human-Computer Studies*, 50, 263-286.

Mayhew, D. J. (1992). *Principles and Guidelines in Software User Interface Design*. Prentice-Hall.

Millward, L. J. (1995) in G. M. Breakwell, S. Hammond and C. Fife-Schaw (Eds.). *Research Methods in Psychology*. Sage.

Mountford, S.J. (1990). Tools and techniques for creative design. In B. Laurel (Ed.) (1990), *The Art of Human-Computer Interface design*. Addison-Wesley.

Muller, M.J. and Czerwinski, M. (1999). Organizing usability work to fit the full product range. *Communications of the ACM*, 42, (5), 87-90.

Muller, M.J., Wildman, D.M. and White, E.A. (1993). Taxonomy of PD practices: a brief practitioner's guide. *Communications of the ACM*, 36, (4), 26-28.

Mullet, K. and Sano, D. (1995). *Designing Visual Interfaces*. SunSoft Press, Prentice Hall.

National Westminster Bank PLC (1999). Company information leaflet about Usability Services Department.

Newman, W. M. and Lamming, M. G. (1995). *Interactive System Design*. Addison-Wesley.

Nielsen, J. (1993). *Usability Engineering*. AP Professional.

Nielsen, J. (1994). Estimating the number of subjects needed for a thinking aloud test. *International Journal of Human-Computer Studies*, 41, 385-397.

Nielsen, J. and Mack, R. L (1994). *Usability Inspection Methods*. Wiley.

Nielsen, J. and Molich, R. (1990). Heuristic evaluation of user interfaces. In: *Proc. CHI '90 Human Factors in Computing Systems*, Seattle, WA, April 1-5, 249-256. ACM/ SIGCHI.

Nisbett, R.E., and Wilson, T.D. (1977). Telling more than we can know: verbal reports of mental processes. *Psychological Review*, 84, 231-259.

Norman, D. A. (1998a). *The Design of Everyday Things*. MIT Press. (Originally published in 1988 as *The Psychology of Everyday Things*, Basic Books).

Norman, D. A. (1998b). *The Invisible Computer*. MIT Press.

Phillips, C.H.E. (1994). Review of graphical notations for specifying direct manipulation interfaces. *Interacting with Computers*, 6, (4), 411-431.

Preece, J., Rogers, Y., Sharp, H., Benyon, D., Holland, S. and Carey, T. (1994). *Human-Computer Interaction*. Addison-Wesley.

Preece, J., Rogers, Y. and Sharp, H. (2002). *Interaction Design: Beyond Human Computer Interaction*. Wiley.

Race, P. (1999). *How to Get a Good Degree*. Open University Press.

Ravden, S. and Johnson, G. (1989). *Evaluating Usability of Human-Computer Interfaces: A Practical Method*. Ellis Horwood Ltd.

Reed, P., Holdaway, K., Isensee, S., Buie, E., Fox, J., Williams, J. and Lund, A. (1999). User interface guidelines and standards: progress, issues and prospects. *Interacting with Computers*, 12, 119-142.

Rettig, M. (1991). Nobody reads documentation. *Communications of the ACM*, 34, (7), 19-24.

Rettig, M. (1994). Prototyping for tiny fingers. *Communications of the ACM*, 37, (4), 21-27.

Rosenfeld, L. and Morville, P. (1998). *Information Architecture for the World Wide Web*. O'Reilly.

Rudd, J., Stern, K. and Isensee, S. (1996). Low vs. high-fidelity prototyping debate. *Interactions*, January, 76-85.

Scane, R. (1987). Verbal protocol analysis and knowledge acquisition. In *Artifact* (University of Southampton publication), pp. 19-22.

Schank, R.C. and Abelson, R. (1977). *Scripts, Plans, Goals and Understanding*. Lawrence Earlbaum Associates.

Sears, A., Jacko, J. A., Chu, J. and Moros, F. (2001). The role of visual search in the design of effective soft keyboards. *Behaviour and Information Technology*, 20, (3), 159-166.

Shepherd, A. (1989). Analysis and training in information technology tasks. In: D. Diaper (Ed.), *Task Analysis for Human-Computer Interaction*. Ellis Horwood Ltd.

Shneiderman, B. (1998). *Designing the User Interface*. Addison-Wesley.

Siegel, S. (1956). *Nonparametric Statistics for the Behavioral Sciences*. McGraw-Hill.

Silcock, N., Lim, K.Y. and Long, J.B. (1990). Requirements and suggestions for a structured analysis and design (human factors) method to support the integration of human factors with system development. In E.J. Lovesey (Ed.) (1990), *Contemporary Ergonomics 1990 (Proceedings of the Ergonomics Society Annual Conference)*. Taylor and Francis, pp. 425-430.

Stammers, R.B. and Shepherd, A. (1995). Task analysis. In: J.R. Wilson and E.N. Corlett (Eds.) *Evaluation of Human Work: A Practical Ergonomics Methodology (2nd Edition)*. Taylor and Francis, pp. 144-168.

Stewart, T. (1999). Overview of standard, aims, objectives, key contents. Presentation at Hawksmere seminar 'ISO 13407 Human Centred Design: making computer systems work for people' Hatton Conference Centre, 28th October 1999.

Stewart, T. (2000). Ergonomics user interface standards: are they more trouble than they are worth? *Ergonomics*, 43, (7), 1030-1044.

Thimbleby, H. and Addison, M. (1996). Intelligent adaptive assistance and its automatic generation. *Interacting with Computers*, 8, (1), 51-68.

Thimbleby, H., Blandford, A., Cairns, P., Curzon, P. and Jones, M. (2002). 'User interface design as systems design'. In X. Faulkner, J. Finlay and F. Détienne (Eds.). *People and Computers XVI – Memorable Yet Invisible. Proceedings of HCI 2002*. Springer.

Torres, R. J. (2002). *Practitioner's Handbook for User Interface Design and Development*. Prentice Hall PTR.

TRUMP. *http://www.usability.serco.com/trump*. Serco is a large, independent usability consultancy in the UK. High quality, extensive information and links relevant to user interface design/usability. (Site last visited 1/4/02.)

Usability Net. *http://www.usabilitynet.org* 'UsabilityNet is a project funded by the EU Framework V IST Programme as IST 1999-29067: a preparatory, accompanying and support measure.' Authoritative, high quality information, papers, links etc. (Site last visited 1/4/02.)

User Interface Engineering. *http://world.std.com/~uieweb/tips.htm* (last accessed 24/11/02). Article 'Making tips work' (2000) Lots of other practical information about user interface design on this website.

van der Meij, H. (1992) A critical assessment of the minimalist approach to documentation. *ACM Tenth International Conference on Systems Documentation*.

van der Meij, H. and Carroll, J. M. (1995) Principles and heuristics for designing minimalist instruction. *Technical Communication*, 2, 243-261.

Vredenburg, K. (1999). Increasing ease of use. *Communications of the ACM*, 42, (5), 67-71.

Wallace, M.D. and Anderson, T.J. (1993). Approaches to interface design. *Interacting with Computers*, 5, (3), 259-278.

Wasserman, A.I. Extending state transition diagrams for the specification of human-computer interaction. IEEE Transactions on Software Engineering, (11), 8, 699-713.

Waterworth, J.A., Chignell, M.H. and Zhai, S.M. (1993). From icons to interface models: designing hypermedia from the bottom up. *International Journal of Man-Machine Studies*, 39, 453-472.

Whitefield, A. and Hill, B. (1994). Comparative analysis of task analysis products. *Interacting with Computers*, 6, (3), 289-309.

Whitefield, A., Wilson, F. and Dowell, J. (1991). A framework for human factors evaluation. *Behaviour and Information Technology*, 10, (1), 65-79.

Wilson, J. R. and Corlett, E. N., (Eds.) (1995) *Evaluation of Human Work: A Practical Ergonomics Methodology* (2nd edition). Taylor and Francis.

Wolfson, S. and Case, G. (2000). The effects of sound and colour on responses to a computer game. *Interacting with Computers,* 13, 183-192.

Index